THE BIG FELLOW

Frank O'Connor — the pseudonym of Michael O'Donovan—was born in Cork in 1903 and educated there at the Christian Brothers School. He worked as a librarian, first in Co. Cork and then in Dublin. He started writing when very young—commencing a collected edition of his own works when he was twelve—and much of his early poetry, stories and translations was published in AE's *Irish Statesman*. His many collections of short stories gained him a world-wide reputation as one of the greatest masters of the form. He died in 1966.

THE BIG FELLOW

Frank O'Connor

PICADOR USA ✻ NEW YORK

Picador® is a U.S. registered trademark and is used by St. Martin's Press under license from Pan Books Limited.

Library of Congress Cataloging-in-Publication Data

O'Connor, Frank, 1903–1966.
     The big fellow / by Frank O'Connor.—1st Picador
USA ed.
          p.   cm.
     Previously published: London : Corgi, 1969.
     Includes index.
     ISBN 0-312-18293-7 (hc)
     ISBN 0-312-18050-0 (pb)
     1. Collins, Michael, 1890–1922.   2. Ireland—
History—Civil War, 1922–1923—Biography.
     3. Ireland—History—Easter Rising, 1916—Biography.
     4. Revolutionaries—Ireland—Biography.
     I. Title.
DA965.C60244   1998
941.5082'2—dc21   97-33373
                                                        CIP

First published in U.S.A. in 1937. Revised edition published in 1965 by Clonmore & Reynolds Ltd. This edition first published in the United Kingdom in 1991 by Poolberg Press Ltd.

First Picador USA Edition: March 1998

10   9   8   7   6   5   4   3   2   1

ACKNOWLEDGMENTS

I am painfully conscious of the inadequacy of an acknowledgment such as this, of the hospitality, the kindness, and often the quite considerable assistance I have received from Collins' friends, many of whom are now dead. Particularly do I feel its inadequacy when it concerns Colonel Joseph O'Reilly and Dr. Richard Hayes. I am much indebted also to Messrs. Frank Aiken, Robert Barton, Piaras Beaslai, Ernest Blythe, Colonel E. Broy, Sean Collins, W. T. Cosgrave, Craig Gardner and Co., Liam Devlin, George Gavan Duffy, Eamon Fleming, Thomas Gay, Christopher Harte, Liam Lanigan, Stephen Lanigan, Diarmuid Lynch, Fionan Lynch, Miss Alice Lyons, Patrick MacCrea, George MacGrath, Mrs. Helen MacGovern, Sean MacEoin, Richard Mulcahy, Fintan Murphy, Mrs. Fintan Murphy, David Neligan, Michael Noyk, Mrs. Batt O'Connor, Florence O'Donoghue, P. S. O'Hegarty, Patrick O'Keeffe, Ernest O'Malley, Colm O'Murchu, Gearoid O'Sullivan, Frank Saurin, Frank Thornton and Liam Tobin.

F. O'C.

Contents

FOREWORD

THIS BOOK has been a labour of love. To some extent it has been an act of reparation. Since the fever of the Civil War died down I have found myself becoming more and more attracted by Collins as a character. For a while I toyed with the idea of a novel. I continued to hear anecdotes of him, and again and again I was struck by their extraordinary consistency. I can remember well the occasion when anecdotes became something more. My friend and colleague, Mr. Gay, was speaking to me of Collins, and so finely did he recreate his dead friend that for the first time I seemed to see Collins as a living man. Half a dozen times since I have caught the same thing from others of his friends, and each time it was as though a ghost had walked in. Those friends of his will, I feel sure, forgive me for blurring that sense of the living man. It is something which is part of their experience and scarcely to be communicated; what catches fire in speech rings cold in print: exaggeration, false emphasis, creep in; yet I should think it a greater loss if that image of the living man, however broken, were lost, than if all the documentation concerning him were to disappear. How often we would sacrifice a hundred studio portraits for one snapshot!

And here a word of warning. Anecdote preserves the living man, but it exaggerates him. When the documents are published it will be seen that Collins was a much greater figure than was suspected by any but a few. But the greater part of Collins' life is in those papers. For a few moments each day he was the schoolboy, the good companion, the great friend, but for the rest of the time he was the worker, and to deal with him without dealing exhaustively with that work scants the respect due to his industry, his patience, good humour and splendid intellect. To give a complete picture of the man one would need to weight down the brilliant sensitive temperament

9

as he himself weighted it, with a mass of arduous and scrupulous labour. But documents—bless them!—have a habit of surviving, and how much of the living man has perished even now I do not care to think.

I have written not for Collins' contemporaries but for a generation which does not know him except as a name. His friends are properly jealous of his reputation, but sometimes in safeguarding reputations we lose something a thousand times more valuable—the sense of a common humanity. A new generation has grown up which is utterly indifferent to the great story that began in Easter 1916. It is even bored by it. We may rage, but can we really expect young people to be interested in the utterly unhuman shadows we have made of its heroes? They don't drink, they don't swear, they don't squabble; they never make fantastic blunders, one is never less wise, urbane and spiritual than the others, they address one another with the exquisite politeness of Chinese mandarins. We, alas, go on drinking, swearing, fighting and making mistakes, and so have no time to spare for this cloudy pantheon of perfect and boring immortals.

I have taken no pains whatever to conceal the fact that Collins was a human being, that he took a drink, swore and lost his temper. It is not as though there were anything to conceal. The worst one can say of him is so trifling that only a mean spirit would distort it to decry him. Without that worst the best rings false, and with Collins the best is always well worth telling.

At any rate it would be a poor compliment to so great a realist. It is as a realist Collins will be remembered, and as a realist he should be an inspiration to the new Ireland. From the Civil War and the despair that followed it sprang a new honesty in Irish life and thought. The old sentimentalism against which Collins almost unconsciously strove has suffered.

I have to acknowledge my deep indebtedness to those authors who have permitted me to make use of their work. I name especially Mr. Piaras Beaslai, whose monumental life of Collins should be read as a corrective to mine; Mr. Pakenham, now the Earl of Longford, whose brilliant analysis of the

Treaty negotiations, *Peace by Ordeal*, I have shamelessly pillaged; Dr. P. MacCartan, who allowed me to make use of his *With De Valera in America*; and Miss Dorothy Macardle, who very generously lent me the proofs of her book *The Irish Republic*, without which I should have found it almost impossible to deal with anything like adequacy with the last period of Collins' life. There are several other books which have been of service to me: Mr. Batt O'Connor's moving autobiography *With Michael Collins*; Mr. Charles Dalton's *With the Dublin Brigade* (a beautiful little book which has never received proper praise); Mr. Desmond Ryan's *Remembering Sion*, which contains unforgettable portraits of Collins and other leaders; Mr. Hayden Talbot's *Michael Collins' Own Story*, which contains a great deal of valuable biographical material; Mr. James Stephens's monograph *Arthur Griffith*; Mr. Darrell Figgis' *Recollections of the Irish War*; Major-General Sir C. E. Cullwell's *Field-Marshal Sir Henry Wilson*; Mr. P. S. O'Hegarty's *Victory of Sinn Fein*; Mr. Winston Churchill's *The World Crisis*. In this new edition I have made use of Ernest O'Malley's *On Another Man's Wound* and Rex Taylor's *Michael Collins*, but I have preferred not to re-write.

F. O'C.

PART ONE

LILLIPUT IN LONDON

CHAPTER I

LILLIPUT IN LONDON

ONE cold bright morning in the spring of the year of fate, 1916, a young man in a peaked cap and grey suit stood on the deck of a boat returning to Ireland. He was in his middle twenties, tall and splendidly built, with a broad, good-tempered face, brown hair and grey eyes. His eyes were deep set and wide apart, his nose was long and fine, his mouth well arched, firm, curling easily to scorn or humour. One interested in the study of behaviour would have noted instantly the extreme mobility of feature which indicated unusual nervous energy; the slight swagger and remarkable grace which indicated an equal physical energy; the prominent jowl which underlined the curve of the mouth, the smile which gave place so suddenly to a frown, and that appearance of having just stepped out of a cold bath which distinguished him from his grimy fellow travellers: the uninterested would have passed him as a handsome but otherwise ordinary young Irishman, shopman or clerk, returning from England on holiday.

It was ten years since this young man, Michael Collins, had left his native place in West Cork. A country boy of fifteen, precocious and sturdy, he had taken the train from the little Irish town where for a year he had been put through the mysteries of competitive examination. With his new travelling bag and new suit, which included his first long pants, he had crossed the sea and passed his first night in exile amid the roar of London.

The boat crept closer to the North Wall. He saw the distant mountains heaped above the city, its many spires, its dingy quays. Everywhere the bells were calling to Mass. It might have been the same Dublin of years before, but beneath it was a different Dublin and a different Ireland. Then it had

15

been butter merchants, cattlemen, labourers who chatted with the manly youth with the broad West Cork accent. Now it was soldiers returning on leave from the wars, some lying along the benches, their heads thrown to one side, their rifles resting beside them, while others, too excited to rest, paced up and down the deck, glad another crossing was over without sight of the conning tower of a submarine. He chummed up with two of them. Some time soon he felt that, instead of chatting with them, he would be fighting them.

That was the greatest change. Then there had been no talk of fight. Mr. Redmond, the leader of the Irish race at home and abroad, hook-nosed, spineless and suave—a perfect Irish gentleman—was in Westminster, and all was well with the country. An election was being held in Galway, and there were brass bands and blackthorns, just as in the good old days. There was money to be made, land to be claimed, position to be secured; all Irish nationalism exacted of its servants was an occasional emotional reference to Emmet on the gallows, Tone with his throat cut. Parnell, whose name the lad of fifteen, following his father, had held dear, was dead, and the intellect of Ireland had been driven into the wilderness. The few who could think were asking what was wrong with the country, and giving different answers. Some said it had no literature ('Literature, my bloody eye!' chorused Lilliput indignantly, busy with increasing its bank balance and saving its soul in the old frenzied Lilliputian way); some that it had lost its native tongue; some that Westminster was corrupting its representatives and that they would be better at home; some that the workers were being exploited by Catholic and Protestant, Englishman and true Gael alike; some that the whole organisation of society was wrong, and that it was vain to increase wealth while middlemen seized it all. Against each of these doctrines Lilliput set up a howl of execration, and the intellectuals of one movement were often the Lilliputians of another. So we find the Gaelic Leaguers ranged against the literary men, and the abstentionists against the workers.

That movement of the intelligence, which Lilliput so deeply resented, had taken place because at the end of the preceding

16

century the great Lilliputian illusion had broken down, the belief that one man could restore its freedom to a bookless, backward, superstitious race which had scarcely emerged from the twilight of mythology. It had broken down because the priests had torn Parnell from his eminence, and Lilliput had assented. Sick at heart, the sensitive and intelligent asked what it meant. None said 'Lilliput', none declared that Ireland was suffering for its sins, or that Lilliput must cast out the slave in its own soul. That is not how masses change. And so arose Yeats and Hyde, Griffith, Larkin and Plunkett.

In turn each of these waves of revolt had spent itself. Synge was dead, Larkin beaten, Griffith a name. The war had brought Lilliput back in strength. There was nothing Lilliput liked better than a good vague cause at the world's end—about the Austrian succession, the temporal power or the neutrality of Belgium. Given such a cause, involving no searching of the heart, no tragedy, it can almost believe itself human. In proportion to its population Ireland had contributed more to French battlefields than England itself. Lilliput did not mind if Ireland was still unfree. All in good time. The great jellyfish of Westminster, the invertebrate leader with the hooked nose and cold, mindless face, let slip the one great chance of winning freedom. Without firing a shot or sending a man to the gallows he might have had it, but refrained—from delicacy of feeling. Lilliput is nothing if not delicate-minded. And now, let the war end without war in Ireland, and all that ferment of the intelligence would have gone for nothing. So at least the intellectuals thought, though it is doubtful if a historical process once begun ever fails for lack of occasion.

Michael Collins was coming back to take part in a revolution which the intellectuals felt was their last kick. They were gathering in from the wilderness to which the Parnellite disillusionment had driven them: labourers, clerks, teachers, doctors, poets, with their antiquated rifles, their amateurish notions of warfare, their absurd, attractive scruples of conscience.

It must have been thrill enough for the soul of the young man when the ship came to rest and the gangways went down that faraway spring morning. The ten years of exile were over.

Sweet, sleepy, dreary, the Dublin quays which would soon echo with the crash of English shells. Even a premonition of what was in store for him could scarcely have stirred him more or the shadow of his own coming greatness; even the feeling that, his work done, the Ireland he loved set free, he himself would personify a mass-possession greater even than that Parnell had stood for, and that from his body, struck down in its glory, the intellect of the nation would pass again into the wilderness.

London of pre-war days was a curious training ground for a man who was about to lead a revolution. The Irish in London —except those who stray, who wish to forget their nationality as quickly as possible—stick together, so that, in one sense, London is only Lilliput writ large. One class, one faith, one attitude; the concerts where preposterously garbed females sing sentimental songs to the accompaniment of the harp, boys and girls dance 'The Walls of Limerick' and 'The Waves of Tory' and play a variety of hurling.

But the young men of Collins' day, however their instincts might urge them to resurrect Lilliput in London, did not have to do so. If they did not wish to go to Mass, there was no opinion that could make them; if they wanted to read what in the homeland would be called 'bad books', there was nobody to stop them. Collins was lucky, not only in being bundled into a big city where he did not need to grow old too soon, but in having a sister who encouraged his studiousness.

To the day of his death he remained an extraordinarily bookish man. History, philosophy, economics, poetry; he read them all and was so quick-witted that he needed no tutor. He went to the theatre week by week, admired Shaw and Barrie, Wilde, Yeats, Colum, Synge; knew by heart vast tracts of 'The Ballad of Reading Gaol', 'The Widow in Bye Street', Yeats' poems, and 'The Playboy'. One cannot imagine him doing anything half-heartedly.

Most of the younger Irish, relieved of the necessity for orthodoxy, favoured a mild agnosticism and 'advanced' ideas. Collins, who did nothing in moderation went further; 'If there is a God, I defy him,' he declared on one occasion. With great

18

fire and persuasiveness he discussed such 'advanced' ideas as the evils of prostitution (which he was shrewd enough to know only at secondhand through the works of Tolstoy and Shaw). Already he was being looked upon as a bit of a character, a playboy, and when in that grand West Cork accent of his he rolled out the Playboy's superb phrases about his father's 'wide and windy acres of rich Munster land', or of being 'abroad in Erris when Good Friday's by, making kisses with our wetted mouths', of the Lord God envying him and being 'lonesome in his golden chair', he was Christy Mahon incarnate, who for the fiftieth time was laying his horrid da with a great clout that split the old man to the breeches belt.

But the old da refused to die. In fact his life had never been in danger. When members of his hurling club debased themselves by playing rugby, Collins was the hottest advocate of their expulsion. When a poor Irish soldier appeared among the spectators on the hurling field in uniform, Collins drove him off. When Robinson's *Patriots* was produced in London, Collins went to hoot it, because Robinson dared to suggest that the people of Cork—his Cork—preferred the cinema to a revolutionary meeting. In fact Collins' studiousness was the mental activity of a highly gifted country lad to whom culture remained a mysterious and all-powerful magic, though not one for everyday use. His reading regularly outdistanced his powers of reflection, and whenever we seek the source of action in him it is always in the world of his childhood that we find it. When excited, he dropped back into the dialect of his West Cork home, as in his dreams he dropped back into the place itself, into memories of its fields, its little whitewashed cottages, Jimmy Santry's forge and the tales he heard in it. There was rarely a creature so compact of his own childhood. To literature and art the real Michael Collins brings the standards of the country fireside of a winter night, emotion and intimacy, and that boyish enthusiasm which makes magic of old legends and can weep over the sorrowful fate of some obscure blacksmith or farmer. The songs he loved best, were all come-all-ye's of endless length, concerning Granuaile or the Bould Galtee Boy.

19

Bold and gallant is my name,
My name I will never deny,
For love of my country I'm banished from home,
And they calls me the Bould Galtee Boy.

The student in him found pleasure in Yeats; his turbulent
temperament found most satisfaction in songs like this which
came out of or went back to the life from which he had
sprung; the thing of which he seems to have known nothing
and cared less is the great middle-class world of approximations
and shadows. His nature safeguarded him from the commonplace. If his pal, Joe O'Reilly, sang 'Maire, my Girl', Collins
got up and left the room impatiently. P. S. O'Hegarty quotes
one of his later utterances, and one of extraordinary significance. He made it, O'Hegarty says, with a difficulty in
finding the appropriate words; which is not to be wondered at,
considering that it was his inmost being he was laying bare:

> 'I stand for an Irish civilisation based on the people and
> embodying and maintaining the things—their habits, ways
> of thought, customs—that make them different—the sort of
> life I was brought up in ... Once, years ago, a crowd of us
> were going along the Shepherd's Bush Road when out of a
> lane came a chap with a donkey—just the sort of donkey
> and just the sort of cart that they have at home. He came
> out quite suddenly and abruptly and we all cheered him.
> Nobody who has not been an exile will understand me, but I
> stand for that.'

There were three qualities which marked Collins all his life
long: his humour, his passionate tenderness, his fiery temper
—and who shall say it is not an Irish make-up? Strangers
usually saw the temper first. He was fond of teasing, was
always making a mock of London-born Irish, and on the
hurling field his loud voice pealed out in good-humoured gibes
of ' 'It it, 'Arry!' But when he was teased himself he went up in
smoke. There is no weakness which men spot sooner or of
which they take more advantage. The result was that everyone

made a dead set on Collins. It was the same in conversation. When he put his head in everyone turned on him. He was roared down unmercifully, with the inevitable result that he lost his temper. When things developed into a fight he always got the worst of it. The more he tried to assert himself, the more punishment he got. But his tempers never lasted. They blew over in a few minutes, the very worst of them, and then that handsome face of his lit up with the most attractive of smiles: on no occasion does he seem to have borne the least grudge against anyone, and what might have been dislike became a good-humoured tolerance. No one could bear malice against a man who bore none, who came up smiling every time and took fresh insults and fresh clips on the jaw with a gorgeous fury which remembered nothing of previous ones.

Collins' youth, for a novelist, represents the most fascinating part of his life. In this we see the first threshings of his genius in a world which did not recognise it. Something similar occurs in the life of every great man. There is a gruesome period when his daemon compels him to behave like a genius, and the crowd, sensibly refusing to take it on trust, sets upon him. As a boy clerk Collins behaved as though he owned the Post Office. All he demanded of his pals was that they should recognise him as a great leader of men on his own unsupported testimony; they insisted on treating him as no better or wiser or stronger than themselves.

There is always something adorable (afterwards) in the picture of genius throwing itself upon the barricades of reality. That is the real explanation of Collins' anticlericalism. He wanted to lead; he was gregarious and bossy; organised concerts, picnics and dances. One can scarcely imagine him except in company. He drank, though never to excess, and swore with a thrilling capacity for improvisation, and always there was that bubbling humour. W. P. O'Ryan tells how he once refereed a ladies' match and threatened to send off one of the girls for using bad language! He was the sort of charming lad who is always trying to sell you tickets for something or other and is cut to the heart when you refuse to buy.

He knew quite early that there was something on in

Ireland, and he wanted to be in it; more than that, he wanted to be prominent in it. When Lanigan took a job in a provincial town nothing would persuade Collins but that he had gone to Ireland in view of an imminent insurrection and that the job was a blind. So, in time, he went himself to Dublin, and got in touch with Tom Clarke and Sean MacDermott, who, having no need of a bùtt, recognised the lad's enthusiasm and energy and gave him work to do in London. Collins was happy at last. A few days before, fresh from Sean and Dublin, he had burst in upon a meeting of the London-Irish, who were discussing sending a deputation to Westminster to protest to Redmond against being conscripted, and warned them to clear back to Ireland as soon as they could. So the little group broke up to meet again in the streets of Dublin.

Now that Collins has become history it is easy for us to see what was most real in him in those London days: the necessity to lead and the love of traditional life. It is the donkey and cart of Shepherd's Bush Road. That donkey and cart was never far from Collins' thoughts: it emerges like a motif in the story of his brief life; sentimental here, jesting there, uncouth and over-boisterous in another place. At the end of his days it is repeated, louder and more menacing, until it assumes a tragic personal significance. It strips off the adopted disbelief; it justifies him when he feels most uncertain of himself; it sets him against his dearest friends in the most sordid wars. He is a man possessed of a boyish loyalty; a vision of white-washed cottages, of old people sitting by the fire, of horses outside the forge on a summer evening. Like all precocious boys he admired older men. Reverence, he said to Hayden Talbot,* was his strongest characteristic. His father was an old man when Collins was born, and the lad worshipped him. One day they were in the field together, the barefooted boy and his father. The father, mounting a fence, pushed loose a heavy stone which rolled towards Collins. He made no attempt to avoid it and watched it until it crushed his instep. He could not believe his father could cause such a thing. 'Great age,' he said to the same biographer, 'held something for me that was

* Talbot: *Michael Collins' Own Story.*

22

awesome. I was much fonder of old people in the darkness than of young people in the daylight.'

In others ideals tend to become abstract. In him the fact of his deep and burning idealism tended to be obscured because it was earthy and tough. Opposed by the superior motives of a Mellowes or de Valera, he is at a disadvantage; clumsy, blundering, giving an impression of disingenuousness; for men and women are notoriously nasty, and abstract principles tenuous and pure, and they live and die austerely if they can be said to live or die at all.

CHAPTER II

UP THE REPUBLIC!

At the top of O'Connell Street stands the red-brown monument to Parnell. Left of it is the Rotunda Hospital, a severe eighteenth-century building with a narrow strip of garden before it. To the right, at the corner of Parnell Street, stood in those days a little tobacco shop which all young Dublin knew.

Inside the counter of the little shop was a little man. He was sixty years of age, spare and spectacled. When you entered he looked at you first over his spectacles and then through them. Sometimes young men came and chattered to him, elbows on the counter; sometimes they retreated into the parlour behind the shop. He favoured young men. They bought Irish cigarettes and went to Irish concerts and dances; they talked Irish, mostly bad. It was all so different to his youth. Then there was no talk of Irish this or that, and though the young men might have heard Irish spoken in their own homes they did not speak it themselves. They were good boys, those of long ago, but these were better. It is a happy old age which can see the world improving.

Yet the world had been hard enough on old Tom Clarke. For sixteen years it had shut him up in English prisons among murderers and thieves. His comrades had gone mad. He, too, might have gone mad but for his indomitable youth. Had he not in the printing shop of the prison, under the eyes of warders and touting prisoners, secretly printed a newspaper, filled with imaginary news—imaginary because he was allowed to know nothing of the world? Had he not, after years, elaborated a means of receiving real news, only to have it snatched from him again? It was a terrible fate, that of Tom Clarke. Even to read of it now, as he described it, with a deep sense of reality so lacking in books by Irish revolutionaries, makes one shudder; but this little old man was able to recreate it all in his mind in the slack hours before sleepy Dublin comes awake, when its streets are like those of a country town, and not only keep his sanity but plan for such another horror in which to end his days.

And the young men would join him. He trusted them, they admired him. They were a queer lot. Several were poets. The young men of Clarke's day had been poets, too, but they wrote things you could understand about 'Dear Old Ireland' and 'Our Martyred Dead'. Plunkett and Thomas MacDonagh wrote English poems that were as foreign to his straightforward mind as the Irish ones of Pat Pearse.

Pearse was a dreamer if ever there was one. He was a mixture of Byron and Oscar Wilde, blended by the pious Catholic teaching of the Christian Brothers. He ran a school outside Rathfarnham, where the boys were taught to resemble the heroes of old sagas. He wrote mostly in Irish, and that deplorable, and was proud of his ability as an orator. His literary efforts show the same blend of fustian and dandyism; they are mannered, morbid and effeminate. To an English father he probably owed the streak of eccentricity. The Dubliners thought him pretentious and a bore.

Thomas MacDonagh was typically Irish; a too-volatile nature, he talked, talked, wrote, wrote, wrote, and talk and verse had the same learned loquacity. An attractive figure, MacDonagh; an adventurer in letters, like a seventeenth-century Irish gentleman in the French or Spanish army; the outline of a great man but without the intellectual substance.

From his fatal facility there emerges but one great poem. His volatile nature permitted him at the end to scoff at mere literature and ask when the poets would settle down to tactics. Dublin, which had sniggered at MacDonagh the poet, did not spare MacDonagh the tactician.

His friend, Joe Plunkett, had travelled a lot. He was even then a dying man; swore by Francis Thompson and G. K. Chesterton, and imitated them with lamentable results. A far greater influence was Sean MacDermott, who remains, when everything has been said, a shadowy, mysterious figure. For the effect he had upon men as mature as Collins, Diarmuid O'Hegarty and O'Sullivan one can show no cause. Apparently he was merely a good-humoured, eager, handsome young cripple with a coaxing tongue, adored by every newsboy in Dublin—as Collins was later to be—his only accomplishment a gift for reciting fiery ballads:

Brian of Banba all alone up from the desert places
Came to stand where the festal throne of the Lord of
*   Thomond's race is . . .*

or:

I am Brian Boy Magee,
My father was Owen Ban,
I was awakened from happy dreams
By the shouts of my startled clan.

Some simplicity of life or thought had given him the mysterious power of swaying men; he was a Pied Piper who lured them after him, and to this day they cannot tell what tune he played.

There were others, though it is doubtful if Collins knew or cared much for them, like James Connolly, whom Æ looked on as the one intellect of the rising. He had had it all planned out for twenty years, and all his socialist activities against the greasy tills of the Martin Murphys had not shaken his determination to have it out with the British Empire too. Arthur

25

Griffith's political writings had had a considerable influence on Collins. He was a stocky, stubborn bourgeois, Connolly's antithesis—frigid with shyness, opinionated, indomitable, incorruptible and lonely. 'Griffith staring in hysterical pride': Yeats' great line places him for ever. His only passion was for music; he could whistle thousands of tunes. He was immensely strong. James Stephens describes going home with him one night and seeing him attacked by a corner boy. He knocked down the corner boy and went on with what he had been saying. It was characteristic of the man's utter imperturbability. On one occasion he mistakenly took a brand-new hat and coat from a rack in the restaurant where he lunched. The owner, a young countryman on his honeymoon, came in great trouble to the men who sat at Griffith's table. As Griffith had never opened his mouth to them, they had no difficulty in persuading the young man that Griffith was a well-known pilferer of coats and hats. 'God, isn't it a cruel world?' the victim said piteously, and then the door opened and Griffith entered. He returned to the rack, took off the coat and hat, put them in their old place, donned his own and disappeared in the same awful silence. Not a smile! Not an apology! A man of iron but utterly without the capacity for leadership, he sought desperately for someone who would implement his ideas.

The young man he was seeking was in Dublin, staying at his friend Belton's farm with a relative by marriage, Sean Hurley, and others of the refugees from conscription. Belton was hospitable, but it irked Collins to be without a job. Most of the London-Irish group had settled in a camp at Kimmage, and he visited them regularly. When he appeared all work stopped and a chorus of voices intoned tauntingly, 'Who killed Mick Collins?' Collins flew into one of his usual rages, and it ended in a free fight, after which everyone was again the best of friends.

In late February he got steady work at Craig Gardner's with his friends Joe and George MacGrath. Even in so short a time he was modifying his opinions. One anecdote has it that, engaged on an audit with a loyalist Protestant firm, he had hot words with one of the clerks. The accountant in charge of the audit was alarmed when he looked out of his office and saw the young firebrand from Cork squaring up to fight. He called him and read him a lecture. As an accountant he should have no politics, he should do his job and avoid political discussions even when provocation was offered. Collins listened obediently, and then a smile broke over his face.

'As a matter of fact,' he said cheerfully, 'it wasn't about politics—only religion!'

Even for Ireland, the Rebellion of 1916 is outstanding for muddle, plot and counterplot, command and countermand, and the utter lack of organising ability at the head. MacNeill's countermanding order has been blamed for the final fiasco, but the real responsibility is on those who adopted the childish plan of concealing things from him. One wonders what the rising would have been like if a great organiser like Collins had been in Ireland for a year or two before; as it is, one can only be grateful that he, too, did not go down in the bloody mess with McDermott and Plunkett.

At noon on Easter Monday they set out for the General Post Office. Collins had passed the previous night in a city hotel with his chief, Joe Plunkett. The day began badly for him. The London-Irish contingent from Kimmage was lined up outside Liberty Hall, and great indeed was their surprise when among the leaders, in the full uniform of a staff captain, appeared their old friend, Mick Collins. The temptation was too great. They began to make fun of him. Collins went white and clenched his fists.

The guard on the G.P.O. was taken by surprise and surrendered, the little group of civilians was seized and bundled out; the Volunteers drove their rifle butts through the windows and barricaded them and proceeded to provision their headquarters from the hotel across the street where Collins had passed the previous night. A little crowd, which included some mystified metropolitan policemen and a few soldiers on leave from the front, gathered—mocking and gaping. They scattered as a party of outraged lancers rode down O'Connell Street at a gallop. They were met by a volley from the new barricaded windows; some horses stumbled and two men crashed on to the cobblestones near the Nelson Pillar. The tricolour appeared on the roof and was greeted by a feeble cheer from the street. An officer—it was Patrick Pearse— appeared and read a proclamation to the re-formed crowd of gapers. The Republic was in being.

The Republic was in being. The citizens of the Republic heard the news with astonishment. The crapulous women leaning out of fourth-storey windows in the spring sunlight yelled questions to the ladies in bonnets and shawls who raced by below. The underworld stumbled down the high staircases of old Georgian mansions, heads began to emerge at street level from basements to which the sun never penetrates. The sitters on the broad stone steps sprang into unwashed activity, surprise and rage mingling in them. Their sons, husbands, brothers, were at the front, fighting the Germans; the separation money flowed like water through the streets, and now the dirty pro-Germans were attacking it. Attacking the blessed separation money!

They crowded in on O'Connell Street, thousands of them, a winning sight for idealists. Now and then a Volunteer sentry fired over their heads and they scurried back with adenoidal shrieks, only to return in a few minutes in greater force.

It was a little while before they recognised the advantages of the new dispensation. Then some rough drove his heel through the window of a sweetshop. Jars of sweets were passed out and distributed generously. Holiday came in the air. Meanwhile uniformed dispatch riders rode up and down the street on their motor bicycles, and cars were seized from their astonished owners.

Within, everyone was strung up, expectant. Connolly, with the irascible efficiency of the old Trades Union leader, had bagged an office and busied himself with the secretary and typists. Collins equally efficient, emptied two tierces of porter down the canteen drain. 'They said we were drunk in '98,' he commented, 'they won't be able to say it now.' Old Clarke, harassed and excited, was blaming everyone for the mistakes which had been made. Poor Clarke had waited so long, he may well be excused. Pearse was enduring a melancholy he could not shake off, and which was made worse by the fact that now the great day had come he had nothing in particular to do but 'speak to the people', as his phrase was for those periodical moody addresses. Another sad figure was O'Rahilly. The leaders, ignoring his great sacrifices, his quixotic nobility, had distrusted him, they had not informed him of the rising, so labelled a poltroon, he came, but communicated with Pearse and the others only through his subordinates. He was a constant reproach to Pearse. 'What a fine man he is!' he exclaimed sadly to Desmond Ryan.

The sound of pick and shovel could be heard eating their way through the rear walls towards Moore Street, in accordance with the Connolly theory of street fighting. The men in eager voices discussed the rumours which were about, that the Germans had landed and the country was up. The women were working downstairs in the basement; there was rice for tea. The London-Irish rowed with Desmond Fitzgerald, who refused them rations without a chit; and Collins, all his rancour against them forgotten, took their part. He had begun to take down the names, addresses and rank of the men on his own landing—the most efficient officer in the whole building, someone called him.

They could hear the crowds in the street outside shrieking ever more wildly as shop front after shop front caved in and goods of every description were passed out. Old women raced away on dancing slippers to get their share of something else. MacDermott came looking for pickets to scatter them. Behind their howling the noise of the city had fallen still. Not a tram, not a car, except some Volunteer car from the country.

Scarcely had they changed guard for the night than the first fire broke out, immediately across the road. The looters had simply set the shell alight, and to the macabre scene, within, where some men watched over the sandbagged windows and some lay about the floor asleep, was added the grotesqueness of the crimson light that bloomed and faded and hissed against the high empty windows through which the cold spring wind came unhindered. Collins and his friend O'Sullivan spent the night in the corridor outside the office in which MacDermott,

Plunkett and Clarke were catching a rest. They ate hard-boiled eggs, and Collins growled at the cackling women who might break the leaders' sleep.

All night long the looting continued. While Volunteers broke in a cycle shop for material for barricades the crowds went about their own business, not so calmly but far more thoroughly, until early morning, when they went singing home to bed and left the city's heart comparatively quiet.

Next day, Tuesday, was almost a repetition of the first. Above the Post Office, women and children used the deserted street as a park in which to take their ease and compare their looted treasures. The rain came, they scooted for shelter, the Volunteers on the roof came down drenched; all over the city they shivered behind their barricades. Another fire began and roared skyward. All night, fire, fire! The sentries on the roof saw what seemed to be the end of their city.

On Wednesday the shelling of Liberty Hall began and English reinforcements poured in. But they met Eamon de Valera's men at Mount Street Bridge and sustained the heaviest casualties of the Rebellion. Connolly was still confident. He was almost alone in his confidence. On Thursday, in his impatient way, he went out with his men on some trifling job and received a bullet in the thigh. Reinforcements were still coming for the British, none for the Irish. Pearse made one of his usual speeches; it was all he could do, now that the forces of reality were loose. Some of the men still kept up a good heart. The rumour of a German landing was still there to comfort them. Pearse sent men on the roof to listen for German gunfire in the bay. These consolations meant nothing to the young realist, Collins. He was enjoying himself, but not because of any illusion about eventual success. The Volunteers were wearing rosary beads and scapulars about their necks. Even this consolation he did not share. 'I'm the only man in the whole place that wasn't at Confession and Communion,' he declared. Except for MacDermott, he had no great belief in the efficiency of the leaders. He could see their mistakes. He could see their helplessness faced by the consequences of those mistakes. Overpowered by a feeling of responsibility for the lives of the men under his command, Pearse mooned about disconsolately from post to post, discussing the theological rights and wrongs of it. The rising had brought forth a new Pearse. He was a dreamer faced with the realisation in action of his dreams—infinitely kind, gentle, approachable, praising O'Rahilly, soothing a wounded English soldier. Collins teased him good-naturedly. He didn't think this was a time for scruples. On all those leaders, Collins, the most loyal of men, would ever after preserve a discreet silence, but Collins, the realist could not shut his eyes to the human weakness which reduced this most gallant of ventures to a wistful tragi-comedy.

·Yet he was very pleased with himself. It was what he had asked for. He was in his element, blustering, joking, encouraging. And the position was desperate enough. The women were evacuated on Friday morning. Shells crashed along the doomed street, the great houses burst into flames. The roof itself took fire and men fell, struck by the first shrapnel.

That night headquarters was evacuated. The men followed the tunnel which had been bored through the shops lining Henry Street. Here a desperate charge was necessary to cross the street under fire. The men crouched against the wall. Connolly, from his stretcher, raved at them. Revolver drawn, Collins emerged and, shouting encouragement to the others, plunged into it head down.

They tunnelled once more. They knew the game was up. Connolly was wounded, O'Rahilly dead on the roadway outside. Collins had concealed a bottle of whiskey. He and his friends, Fionan Lynch and Jim Ryan, smoke-begrimed and grim, drank, as it seemed, for the last time together.

On Saturday the surrender was inevitable. Pearse's scruples had outgrown every other consideration of him. Clarke alone wished to hold out. MacDermott went from post to post weeping. The Pied Piper had summoned them out to this carnival of blood, and now his magic had deserted him. His pipe was broken, his last tune played.

Not quite yet though. The London-Irish, desperate at the thought that for them surrender meant only conscription and further horrors, had met in a battered cottage in Moore Lane and decided to fight it out. Collins came upon them when their minds were made up. He saw the danger, that if they continued to fight it would only mean a greater certainty of death for the unfortunate leaders. He argued, entreated, but they would not yield, so, in despair, he went off for MacDermott. MacDermott fascinated them as he had already fascinated so many other young men. 'We'll die,' he said simply. 'You will escape. No one will try to conscript you.'

At two o'clock Pearse surrendered unconditionally, and Collins marched out with the others to lay down his gun. One story describes him looking back at the Post Office and saying with a toss of the head, 'The flag is still flying anyway.' Corpses littered the pavements. They were marched between the long files of soldiers to the Rotunda Hospital. It was an apocalyptic scene: the blazing thoroughfare, the lines of English soldiers in trench helmets, the Red Cross cars whirring by, and the few hundred bandaged, grimy, desperate men on their way to what seemed certain death. Old Clarke, defiant and erect, MacDermott limping, tap-tapping with his stick. From the garden behind the high metal railings and rows of fixed bayonets the blazing street still confronted them. The corner shop at the left-hand side was English headquarters—the little tobacco shop of the old Fenian, where it had all begun in some terribly distant past when Dublin was still a sweet, dull, dreary English provincial town. And there was old Tom himself, a prisoner again, not fifty yards from the little shop where he had sold *Tit-Bits* and Wild Woodbines to the soldiers who were now guarding him.

Once they were disarmed there was no more politeness. One officer strode up and down among them, mocking, cuffing, beating them. Half mad with rage, he picked them out one by one. 'Don't smoke! Don't stand up! Don't lie down!' He dragged out old Clarke and stripped him naked. Collins shouted in protest; he, too, was dragged out and cuffed; O'Sullivan, giving his name in Irish, was struck, and Joe O'Reilly. But they were helpless, Collins, who had a long memory, remembered not his own humiliation, for he never remembered such things, but the humiliation of old Clarke.

There would be a day of reckoning for that, and then there would be no more romantic outbursts which left them to the mercy of sadistic savages. It was the savages who would go in fear, and one fine spring morning that gallant officer would meet a most unromantic end in a quiet road in County Wexford.

Night fell. As the other outposts surrendered, fresh contingents of prisoners arrived. They were crowded one on another till there was scarcely room to stand. The night turned colder and a slow, drenching rain began to fall, but still the heart of the city burned. In the cold dawn they saw one another's faces. Not often does such a dawn of despair come to young romantics; British soldiers were digging a giant grave. How many of them would fall into it they did not know. They were marched through the ruined streets to Richmond Barracks, where the political detectives of the Dublin Metropolitan Police pounced on them. It was Collins' first intimate experience of a force with which he was to have quite a lot to do. He saw his leaders picked out for death and penal servitude. No one picked him out, for the face of the lad from London was still unfamiliar; he had not spoken at political meetings or marched with the Volunteers. In the tragic irony of this tale there is an especial irony in the fact that the detectives left behind them the only really dangerous man, the man who, within a few short years, would kill off the craftiest of them and render the rest so impotent that he would be able to walk the streets of Dublin undisguised. Not without irony, too, the plight of one detective who whispered to prisoner after prisoner, 'Can I do anything for you? Can I take a message for you?' They all scowled at him, thinking this but another trick, unaware of the conflict of loyalties in the heart of Joe Kavanagh, who would yet be Collins' agent in Dublin Castle.

On the same evening Collins and the rest of the less guilty were taken across channel to cool their heels in Stafford Military Prison, while Pearse, Plunkett, MacDonagh, old Tom Clarke and Collins' idol, Sean MacDermott, remained to face English firing squads.

33

CHAPTER III

JAILBIRDS

MORNING saw them in Holyhead, a place very familiar to the exiles among them. When the train stopped in a station the posters gave them the first news of the suppression of the Rising, and the angry crowds that filled the stations, the measure of England's reaction.

The military detention barracks at Stafford was Collins' first taste of prison. He was a good prisoner, the sort of man who does not find himself helpless before the necessity of washing his floor or polishing his mug. He was the neatest of men, good at washing up, good at darning; he liked the feel of things, and he liked people, so he was a favourite with the Tommies. Not only was he the sort men like, his instinct for leadership gave him the knack of understanding and enjoying the English soldiers. He bantered and bullied them in a way they liked. But he had also a genius for managing things, and within a day or two he succeeded in establishing communication with his neighbours.

After three weeks the cell doors were flung open, and prisoners rushed to exchange impressions. Only then did they realise the fate that had overtaken their leaders. Collins felt intensely the loss of MacDermott. But they were young men who for weeks had been cooped up in tiny cells, and there was a world of freedom to be taken advantage of. First off the mark was Collins, always eager to exercise, playing games with an improvised ball, wrestling, boxing, teasing, carrying out endless practical jokes. He had neither lost nor learned to conceal his temper. No sooner had he got possession of the raggy ball than there was a mass charge and he was borne down, cursing and swearing, to emerge a few minutes later with his face flushed and his hair wild. They fled before him with hoots of glee.

In the prison he was rarely at rest but prowled up and down with a gang of wild youths like himself, looking for someone to tease or manhandle. He was always bursting with high spirits. When he had forced a man into submission he rose with a wild crow of delight and looked for someone stronger. He never admitted defeat himself; there were prisoners who could put him through it, but one defeat was scarcely over before he came looking for another. When he played cards he did so with great intensity—so long as his hand was good; then he resented interruption. But when his hand was indifferent he tired of the game. He looked into his neighbour's cards, reneged, upset the deck, or created a diversion by dragging the most likely looking winner on to the floor. It was the same with beds and other possessions; so long as they were someone else's they were there for his amusement, but let no one dare to interfere with his! His strength made him fairly safe from individual attack, so his enemies were forced to come in numbers.

That was how many of his companions became acquainted with their future leader. It is small wonder if the more thoughtful paid no attention. In prison the full-blooded, swearing, schoolboy type is an unmitigated nuisance. Only a few found that Collins had a wide literary background—though with the athlete's self-consciousness he dismissed it in a slangy phrase—or that he spent a portion of each day in study. It cannot be too much emphasised that he remained all his life a student, ready to learn from anyone, but his studies were always practical. Practical in the sense that they came home to him. He studied not only French, which might be useful to him as a clerk, but Irish and Irish history.

To Collins the relief at being transferred to an internment camp was enormous. Frongoch Camp, where he found himself next, was divided into two parts: the South Camp, which consisted of an old distillery, and the North—Collins' quarters —of huts. His hut, as one might expect, was the noisiest in the compound. The inhabitants were never done with wrestling, pillow fighting and so on. Still Collins, who was first up in the mornings, succeeded in escaping and continuing his studies.

Here, too, he showed the first signs of that ability for getting

35

the practical things done. With the mistaken notion that thereby they would frighten the guards from contact with the prisoners, the British had put it about that they were financed by German gold. Gold is a dangerous subject to mention before men as poor as the average Tommy, and individual prisoners were asked by their guards if they were the men who gave money to soldiers. Collins took advantage of the occasion to establish a line of communication with the outside world.

But the most important thing that occurred in Frongoch was the reorganisation of the Irish Republican Brotherhood, which had been mainly responsible for the Rising. In this reorganisation Collins played a leading part, and to the backing of this secret society can be traced the startling suddenness with which an unknown lad from Cork later established his ascendancy over the whole revolutionary movement.

Frongoch represented one long row with the English authorities regarding the refugees. In Moore Lane, before the surrender, MacDermott had prophesied that, though he and his companions would die, they would go unharmed, but with characteristic stupidity the army authorities decided that they must be conscripted. Collins, whom they looked upon as their adviser, counselled them to withhold their names, and in this many others joined them. Those who refused were sent to the South Camp for punishment, and Collins tried to go too. A burly sergeant hurled him out of the ranks with, ' 'Ere, Collins, get out! We all knows you!' This unfuriated him. He hated being left out of a good scrap. He contrived to establish communication with them and sent them cigarettes and food out of his own scanty supplies.

On the second occasion he was luckier and managed to get accepted among the malcontents. He fixed up communications as usual, and cigarettes and food once more began to trickle in. Collins distributed them. The result was that he often went without cigarettes himself. This was not only his fabulous natural generosity, it was partly his need for leadership. He was the sort of man who would willingly have allowed himself to be cut in pieces for those who once acknowledged it. Always there is the necessity to prove himself better, cleverer, stronger

36

than the rest; it is in his studiousness, in his skill at athletics. He must triumph, and when he does there is a sort of innocent boyish glory about him. He was first-rate at the high jump, the hammer throwing and the hundred yards. O'Reilly describes how he had almost won the hundred yards when he suddenly saw Collins go past him, and as he did he hissed gleefully, all his face a grin of delight, 'Ah, you whore, you can't run!' This was the occasion when, in answer to a question regarding the treatment of prisoners, a suave cabinet minister quoted his running time as an indication of the way in which they were looked after.

With the 'forward' group and most of the young men Collins was on good terms, and they accepted him without thinking him in any way remarkable, but with the older men and the moderates generally he was on very uneasy terms. They disliked his thrusting ways—his demand for more and more violent methods. All temperament, he made no attempt to conceal his feelings towards them; with a scowl, a thrust of the jaw, a toss of the head, he called them to their faces, 'cowards', 'bloody lousers', 'ould cods', and other names even less likely to endear him to them. It gave him a reputation he would find hard to live down, as an extremist whom nothing would satisfy.

His companions summed up the side of him they most disliked in one scornful phase—the Big Fellow! 'Collins thinks he's a big fellow,' they repeated. The nickname stuck; henceforth he was the Big Fellow, and the story of his brief life is the story of how he turned the scornful nickname into one of awe and affection.

He was nine months a prisoner when the general release came. He arrived back in Dublin on Christmas morning 1916. He and O'Sullivan burst in the locked door of the room which Joe O'Reilly was sharing with a friend, looking for 'a bit of ear'. 'A bit of ear' was the goal of all Collins' wrestling matches. Having bitten O'Reilly's ears till they bled, pinched and savaged him and emptied part of a bottle of port down his throat, they left him to explain to his terrified room-mate that this was merely Collins' idea of fun. That evening he was lifted on to a side-car and, drunk as a lord, bundled by his friends into the Cork train.

CHAPTER IV

RAINBOW CHASERS

WHEN Collins returned to Dublin in the New Year, the younger men who had been interned with him were already beginning to reorganise the movements which had been shattered by the revolution—the Volunteers and the Republican Brotherhood. In turn, the Brotherhood set about gaining control of such organisations as might prove useful. One of these was the National Aid Association, which collected and distributed a relief fund for the victims of the rising. The association had considerable resources, and the young conspirators felt they might well be applied to purposes not so strictly charitable. Collins, now a member of the Supreme Council, having shown a real flair for intrigue and a great deal of energy, was selected for this job and appointed secretary.

He was, as might be imagined, an excellent one. Though his salary was less than that of the average clerk, he put into the work his whole passion for efficiency and organisation. Before that, people had crowded and gossiped in the cramped space of the little office. Now they found themselves faced by a formidable counter and an equally formidable young man with a big jowl, who showed no pleasure in the Irish pastime of bandying words. Some did not like the change. It wasn't only that the young man was efficient; he was also truculent; as might have been expected of the Collins who had irritated the moderate of Frongoch, he was lacking in urbanity and threw his weight about.

His efficiency and enthusiasm took unexpected forms. Among his bosom friends he sold National Aid, and when they called for drinks and produced ten-shilling notes to pay, he diverted attention by some amusing anecdote while he coolly pocketed the change. Next morning they received an official receipt by post. Even those who liked him least had to admit that he worked. Often they saw him cycling home at midnight, having completed his rounds. It was never too late or too far for him if there was someone in trouble. Nor did he assist only with the Association's funds. When ordinary sources failed, he contrived to help some of the down and outs of the Rising out of his own miserable salary.

It was a job ideally suited to his genius and his character. As Beaslai points out, it brought him into contact with all the most vital figures and helped him to form that unerring vision, not of city or country but of the whole nation. And more important still, it fitted in well with and reinforced his natural bent towards realism. In prison he had found that English guards could be bribed; as secretary of the National Aid Association he could see that even Irish patriots know the miseries of poverty, and how they break the human spirit. He did not have to look far to find that out. There came to him in his office men who had fought beside him in the General Post Office and played football with him in Frongoch, now practically destitute and glad of even the few shillings he could spare them. He was the most warm-hearted of men with what for such a healthy animal can only be described as an extraordinary refinement of emotion, and even a hint of poverty, loneliness, illness or old age was sufficient to bring tears to his eyes and rouse all that was most combative in him. He put an end to one budding romance when the girl argued that a woman was justified in breaking her engagement to a man with an incurable disease. In the theatre what he liked best was tragedy; burlesque of any sort he abhorred. It is a trait characteristic of a certain noble approach to life; it is the same 'reverence' of which he spoke to Hayden Talbot. Violence, which came naturally to him, he permitted himself only with the young, men and women; old people and children he was always gentle with. That strange romantic tenderness, that sense of the eternal wistfulness of things, made him an ideal secretary for such an organisation. One can never think of him as being superior; he was the man of all others most likely to rob charity of its sting. If ever he had in his make-up even a hint of the idealist's niggardliness, this job cured it; for ever after, and sometimes with the most unfortunate results, he erred on the side of lavishness.

The National Aid Association was lucky in its secretary, but the whole political organisation was in complete muddle. In February 1917 an election was held in Roscommon. Collins worked on it on behalf of Plunkett, the father of his executed chief, and on snowy winter days made fiery speeches in little country towns and villages. Emotion at the executions and imprisonments had shaken a large minority of the people, but the parliamentary machine of the Irish Party—firmly embedded in the apathy, the dull-witted utilitarianism, of everyday life in Ireland—was still immensely strong. Brazen-tongued, brainless, insolent and sordid, it challenged every ideal, and the young orators replied with naked emotion and violent romanticism. The fight which was being waged in the slush of those January days in Roscommon would soon transfer itself to every corner of Ireland.

Plunkett was elected. He was a minor poet who had been at one time a British loyalist, so loyal that Griffith, out of a lifetime of impoverished integrity, distrusted him. But Collins' secret organisation equally distrusted Griffith, whose maximum claim was the restoration of the independence enjoyed by the Old Irish Parliament of Grattan's day, which he believed could be won by moral force without recourse to arms. These theories were equally anathematised by the extremists. For the next few years the intrigue of Collins and the I.R.B. was directed to keeping out the moderates, and there went on what can only be described as an underground war between Collins and Griffith—an extraordinary conflict which was seldom externalised and has never been chronicled.

Plunkett's idea was to start a new organisation which would swallow up Griffith's Sinn Fein party. Griffith, stocky and tenacious, hung on and refused to have his organisation dislodged—luckily for the country, which was in a state of frenzy and ready for any folly.

In May there was another election in Longford. Collins, still suffering from the effects of his experiences in Roscommon, threw himself into it, organised, made speeches, caroused—and fell in love. Here he found a second home, and after this episode Longford was linked in his mind with Cork. It meant more to him than it might have meant to another; till his death he was to have no home; he who adored children would never play with his own children at his own fireside; the romance which his ardent temperament cried out for was denied him. From his favourite book he would quote with shining eyes the story of Wolfe Tone's courtship of the demure young lady of Grafton Street, but Tone's immortal romance was to have no parallel in his own life.

The following month produced the release from prison of the remaining captives of the Rising and the election of one of them as member for East Clare. This man, Eamon de Valera, the revolutionaries at home had selected almost blindfold as their leader. He was the only senior officer who had escaped the firing squad; his troops had put up the toughest fight of all; he had cried out at the surrender that the people should have come out and fought with knives and forks. Here surely, they thought, was an extremist with whom they could beat Griffith, Plunkett, the politician and anyone who might possibly be classed as a moderate. They had chosen unaware an extraordinary character, perhaps the most extraordinary the Revolution threw up. Tall, thin, sallow, with a drooping mouth set in firm lines and a colourless face which rarely smiled, de Valera had been an unnoticed teacher of mathematics before the Rising.

But the country was frenzied; it pushed this way and that, helplessly, blindly, seeking a leader—any sort of a leader, if only he would show it how to hit back. It was this obscure desire to hit back which put any moderate out of question and gave the secret organisation its chance. Speakers who wished to please the crowd, which had suddenly grown conscious of its own impotence before the whim of an English general, must talk guns; singers at the public concerts, which had now grown popular, must sing treason. There were many concerts, many meetings, and the police banned them; and the crowds, seeking to outwit them, hurried here and there in the darkness. The police batoned like madmen, the flying crowds retorted with showers of stones, but the young men, their fingers itching for a trigger, raged and waited, waited and raged. It was an extraordinary period, its literature the ballad sheet, its music the wavering chorus of crowds, choked with emotion. One remembers it is an emotional maelstrom; dark nights, dark excited faces flying before the charge of armed policemen.

Speaker after speaker was jailed for the violence of his orations. The Brennans of Clare set a headline by ignoring the magistrate's court which tried them. Fionan Lynch, Austin Stack, Tom Ashe, all intimates of Collins, went to jail, spitting contempt at their judges; and still speakers sprang up, and still the endless spate of words went on. The refusal to recognise the court crystallised into a contemptuous formula.

Then in September words led to something worse. The prisoners went on hunger strike as a protest against being herded with criminals; a brutal official fed them forcibly, and Ashe the handsome, Ashe the romantic, died. It was the first loss Collins had sustained in the new struggle. He was devoted, heart and soul, to his friends, and Ashe was the first of many whose death plunged him into a savage gloom and discouragement. The sense of tragedy was highly developed in him; in Ashe's death he saw the death which was probably awaiting himself.

His mood reflected that of the nation. Ashe, who had shared in the pre-rising taste for bad verse, was transformed overnight into a hero. In every little shop copies of his last poem were sold by the hundred; at every concert reciters rolled it out:

> *Let me carry your cross for Ireland, Lord,*
> *For Ireland weak with tears,*
> *For the aged man of the clouded brow,*
> *For the child of tender years . . .*

Collins, in uniform, delivered a brief and manly oration

42

above the grave of his dead friend. The idea of secrecy was still far from everyone's mind; the Volunteers were still thinking in terms of 1916 and another general rising; of new uniforms and obsolete guns.

Yet, even among those who would not have said no to another despairing fight, Collins was being looked upon as a hotheaded young fool. It is true that he thought a strong word as good as a strong blow. The feeling of distrust on the part of the more levelheaded was intensified during the following month by the tactics which he and his extremist friends of the Republican Brotherhood adopted to force Griffith out of the presidency of Sinn Fein, which, having been fortuitously identified by the English with the Rising of 1916, had secured so much popular sympathy that it remained the only political organisation the country would cotton on to.

Fortunately Griffith, instead of forcing a split which would have resulted in victory for himself, stood down—had he not always maintained he was no leader?—and the new and untried de Valera assumed the leadership of a party which Griffith had founded and, during a lifetime of poverty, sustained. Griffith's old friends were not inclined to forget the young man who had taken so great a part in the shelving of their leader, and the convention expressed its feeling by giving him the very last place on the executive—this in spite of the Volunteer and I.R.B. bloc, which voted as a group for its own leaders. De Valera showed his gratitude by refusing to join the I.R.B. The Volunteers, who held their convention a few days later, were more friendly and gave Collins the job of Director of Organisation, though, as was later shown by the selection of Mulcahy as Chief of Staff, even among the Volunteers, in fact among the extremists themselves, there were men like Dick Mackee who looked on Collins with distrust.

This convention introduces us to two men who were to play a very important part in Collins' life. The then Chief of Staff, Charles Burgess, or Cathal Brugha, as everyone knew him, was one of the heroes of 1916. He had been left for dead at his post, literally riddled with bullets and fighting until the last. He was small, sallow, narrow eyed with a deep upper lip that

43

shuttered his mouth even when he smiled. He was the North Pole to Collins' Equator. While Collins' nature was at boiling point and burst out in earthquakes, thunderstorms and showers, he dwelt amid ice floes and fogs. He was straightforward, rude in dispute, not with Collins' violent emotional rudeness, but calculatedly. As Griffith's adjusting of his tie proclaimed his nervous obstinacy, Brugha's buttoning of his blue reefer jacket expressed his courageous blindness, his boxer's good temper and cheerful readiness to take any God's amount of punishment. He was partner in a candlemaker's, and before the Rising, when he was employed as commercial traveller, had sworn in revolutionaries in every parish in Ireland over a pound of church candles. But their failure in the Rising had so disgusted him that he forswore secret societies and frowned on Collins' reorganisation of the Republican Brotherhood.

Mulcahy, on the other hand, was a born dreamer. He was slow and elaborate in speech, and while he talked his fingers wrote things on the air. Collins' friend Cullen called him the 'Ticktack Man', and the name stuck. He had an extraordinarily attractive face, with piercing blue eyes; the ascetic face of the monk. He was a type which Terence MacSwiney later made familiar, and in this natural asceticism his affinity was with Brugha rather than Collins. Mulcahy, immersed in his own task, worked for years beside Collins, but the acquaintance never ripened into anything more.

CHAPTER V

THE FIRST ROUND

GRIFFITH'S policy of abstention from the English Parliament, which the revolutionaries had nominally adopted, had one grave weakness. To succeed it must be applied wholesale; that necessitated a general election; and the question was, would

44

the temper of the people last? Its pace was far too slow for the Irish temperament; to one with Collins' temperament it must have seemed funereal. Irish people are volatile. They had elected four rebels: that was sufficient to register their protest against the slaying of unarmed Irish poets; now they were beginning to grow concerned over the new bridge they wanted, the new school, the new pier.

Three defeats in quick succession hit the patriots badly. It is true that the constituencies were not ideal ones for a straight fight with the Parliamentarians; two were in Ulster, which is almost entirely inhabited by factionists of one colour or another; one in Redmond's old constituency; but twelve months had barely elapsed since English guns had laid Pearse and his companions in the common grave, and the country could not afford an annual rising.

But luck was on their side. Irishmen dealing with Englishmen are at a disadvantage, but the Coalition had given England Lloyd George, and Lloyd George was an excellent antagonist. He was a Celt. If you hit him he hit back instantly. If you insulted him he lost his temper. The Irish were becoming more and more insulting. Collins got three months in Sligo Gaol for a fiery speech, but Lloyd George, hot and bothered by all this Irish hullabaloo, had something bigger up his sleeve.

In April 1918 he introduced conscription for Ireland and drove the last remnant of the Redmondites—his only real allies—from Westminster. They returned to Dublin, conferred with the patriots whom up to this they had been denouncing as rainbow chasers, and, with the tail of constitutionalism between their legs, repaired with de Valera to Maynooth, where the bishops solemnly blessed the anti-conscription campaign.

Lloyd George's idea of the dictator necessary to impose conscription was Sir John French, and Johnnie, as his intimates called him, was instructed to give the rebels hell. Only one proviso did Lloyd George make—the rebels must be forced to shoot first. In the third week of May that distinguished soldier took up the task of making the rebels shoot first.

The rebels, with Sir John French in prospect, ordered Collins to give bail. He was released at the end of April and drove straight to Granard. The local Volunteers gave him a royal welcome, and he drove through a street lined by men. He spent a day there and returned to Dublin.

It was at this time that Ernie O'Malley met him first at his office in Bachelor's Walk.

'He was pacing up and down. We shook hands. He jerked his head to a chair to indicate that I should sit; he took a chair which he tilted back against the wall. On shelves were green membership cards, heaps of the *Irish Volunteer Handbook*, and stacks of white copies of the organisation scheme. Behind his desk was a large map of Ireland marked with broad red streaks radiating from Dublin. He was tall, his energy showed through rapid movement. A curving bunch of hair fell on his forehead; he tossed it back with a vigorous head twist. . . .

'He pointed out communication routes on the wall map. I was to improve and keep them tested by dispatch riders. He gave me a bundle of organisation schemes, instructions for the preparation of emergency rations, lists of equipment that could be made locally. "Read that and see what you think of it." He handed me notes on the destruction of railways, bridges and engines with and without explosives. It was signed by Rory O'Connor, Director of Engineering. He crossed to the window while I read. "My bail is up," he said. "They're looking for me now." "They" meant the "G" men, who carried out political arrests in Dublin. Collins had been arrested for a Volunteer recruiting speech; he had been released on bail. That was unusual. Volunteers were not allowed to accept bail. Two nights ago "G" men brought off a raid; they found empty packing cases and a pile of cartridge wrappers in a store. Bruton said, "This looks as if there were brains behind it; I bet it's that fellow from Mountjoy Street." Collins laughed; it meant himself.'

It is an excellent picture; the little touch of raw vanity is characteristic of the period.

On the first of May he met Joe O'Reilly in O'Connell Street. O'Reilly had been with him in London, in the Rising, in

46

Stafford and Frongoch, but his fate had been very different to his friend's. For six months he had been kicking about Dublin, without a job. Collins had helped him by securing him a grant from the National Aid Association. A week before, unable to stand any more of it, the lad had taken employment under the British government as a labourer in Tallaght Aerodrome. Collins, in his usual way, began to guy him. Then he suddenly turned serious.

'Chuck it and come in with me,' he said. 'I have a big job in front of me and I'll want help.'

Without a moment's hesitation O'Reilly agreed. All he asked was that he should be allowed to collect what was due to him. Even this Collins refused to allow; he was already testing his ascendancy.

At that moment began the most intimate relationship of his career. O'Reilly, slim, delicate, sensitive, had the stuff of the mediaeval page in him. His devotion to Collins was boundless. No one except O'Reilly himself could do justice to it, or to the strange fragrance of romance which surrounds it and makes one think again of a mediaeval tale. He was courier, clerk, messenger boy, nurse, slave. When Collins was in the mood for relaxation, he sang the old ballads Collins loved; when he was out of sorts, he endured his bad humour. He was out in all weathers on his old bike, shivering and drenched. When the fat and lazy detectives from Dublin Castle had wasted their day in a pub, they simply recorded that they had noticed Joe O'Reilly in College Green. His work was never completed, never rewarded, and beyond it was the shadow of the prison and, later, of the torture room. Yet he went about it singing and joking. He alone could tell where Collins might be at any particular moment and what he was planning, but he knew how to keep his mouth shut.

The conscription menace gave him and his chief a great deal to do. Nothing could have been better calculated to stiffen Sinn Fein. Lilliput had done its best for the sacred cause of Belgium as for the Vatican against Garibaldi, but even in Lilliput there are thousands with no strong desire to sacrifice themselves. Loyalists and rebels were at one in this. Collins had a busy time. Never, if he had recruited a whole lifetime long, could he have hoped to swell the ranks of his little civilian army as in those days of indecision and panic. Outside every chapel in Ireland impressive scenes were witnessed as thousands of men took a pledge to resist conscription to the death. It looked as though Johnnie would have a busy time.

The real effect of the scare was to turn the Volunteers from a political minority into a national army. It was a blow from which Griffith's moderates as well as the old Parliamentarians were never to recover. It was to the Volunteers the terrified civilian population looked for a lead; even the omnipotent priesthood was compelled to defer; and the prestige they gained was something it took a civil war to destroy.

The crisis also forced the leaders of the Volunteers to think ahead, and in terms of attack as well as defence. Collins and his companions were busy with plans for assassinating the English cabinet in the streets of London, and already there were desperate men on watch at Downing Street. It was a change from the time when patriot leaders could think only of armies in uniform with green flags flying. It was a step forward in realism, and for that they owed thanks to Lloyd George.

But French wished to prepare the ground. One day a detective called at the Public Library in Capel Street and asked for the librarian, Gay. He was a tall, slow-moving man with a wife and family, cautious and yet warm-hearted. Some prisoner had given him a message for Gay, and, in his desire to be accepted, he had done other little favours for Gay, such as bringing him Irish-American papers from the Castle. This time what he brought was something more important. It was a long list of patriot leaders who were to be arrested that very night. The detective was our old friend Joe Kavanagh, who had travelled far since that distant day in Richmond Barracks when his task had been to pick out young Irishmen for the firing squad.

Gay, too, was aware of the importance of the occasion. He went straight to Harry Boland, who kept the tailor's shop in Middle Abbey Street. Boland went with the news to his friend

Collins, who was working at an office in Bachelor's Walk. A few days before a similar warning had reached Collins from a young police clerk named Ned Broy, though Broy had given no names. Collins doubted if there was anything in it, but he took no chances. O'Reilly was sent out on his bike with a large number of warnings. A meeting of the Volunteer executive was held that evening, and Collins mentioned it. Paddy O'Keeffe mentioned it at another meeting, this time of the Sinn Fein executive. No action was taken; the Sinn Fein leaders decided to await their arrest. The result was that almost all the leaders, including de Valera, were swept into the police net. A gunboat was waiting at Dunleary, and all that night and all next day the captives were brought aboard. His companions looked in vain for Collins. He had blundered into the raiding parties on his bicycle, rushed off to give warning to the others, and finding that MacGarry's house had been raided and its owner arrested, went comfortably to sleep there, knowing that there at least he would be safe from the police. From this on he stayed mostly at the house of Joe MacDonagh, another victim of the swoop.

Next day Collins was able to make a survey. He may well have cursed. Nearly every leader had gone. There remained himself and Boland. His first action was to send a five-pound note to Joe Kavanagh. Tact was not his strong point. Gay, with a sense of what the occasion demanded, returned it.

'You didn't give him the money,' asked Collins in surprise.

'No,' said Gay.

'You didn't think he'd take it?'

'No.'

'A bloody queer "G" man,' growled Collins.

Collins was born a mighty worker. Now, with the arrest of the leaders, the work was being thrown more and more upon his shoulders. Lloyd George had calculated upon paralysing the Sinn Fein movement as a preliminary to conscripting an army. Instead, he had given Ireland a permanent grievance and the revolutionary movement its ablest leader since Wolfe Tone.

O'Malley gives us another revealing sketch of him at this time:

'Collins was now in St. Ita's, the first school founded by Padraig Pearse. The room was called the dug-out. It had been a cellar of some kind or a storeroom; the door was not easy to find. I had a moustache, a bushy unkempt growth; it changed my appearance, and gave me, I hoped, the weight of age. Somehow a moustache made one more serious-minded. The door was half open; I walked in. Collins was working at a big wooden table, his back to a bare white-washed wall, a pile of addressed envelopes in front of him. He stood up quickly when he saw me. He looked as if he had been taken off his guard. "What the bloody hell" . . . he began. I laughed; he recognised me. I had forgotten about the moustache. He continued to write; the pile of envelopes increased. I watched him; there was envy in my look for I found it hard to make enough work to keep me busy.'

Through the summer of 1918 Collins worked like a devil, at the same time trying to fight off a bad attack of pleurisy. Stephens has told us how Griffith faced an attack of African fever; he woke one morning with the symptoms, took a ball, went to a dead wall near his house, and played handball alone for six hours. Collins' reaction was just as characteristic. He stormed and raged at his illness like a man demented, falling in his tracks with pain. After a short stay in bed he rose and prepared to go out on his bicycle. O'Reilly, in consternation, endeavoured to dissuade him, but he only growled. Whereupon O'Reilly, who was still new to his chief and filled with the most touching romantic devotion, decided to follow him un-observed.

Collins' progress was decidedly wobbly, and outside Store Street police station he collapsed. O'Reilly dashed up, but Collins had already succeeded in raising himself and was gazing stupidly at his machine, which had lost a pedal. When he saw O'Reilly, instead of gratitude he showed every sympton of ungovernable rage.

'Here, Mick,' said O'Reilly, 'take my bicycle. I'll bring yours.'

With difficulty Collins mounted and rode off, but indignation made him turn frequently to glare back at his devoted courier, who was doing his sorry best to keep up on a bicycle which had lost a pedal and which, besides, was suitable only for Collins' long legs. At Cullenswood House he had so far forgotten his ailment in his rage that he threatened to take O'Reilly's life if ever he were followed again. Whereupon he collapsed once more, and O'Reilly, whose romantic conception of his job was undergoing a speedy metamorphosis, rushed out for whiskey.

Collins dragged his way to MacDonagh's house, where he was staying, and was put to bed. Mrs. MacDonagh rubbed his chest. He interspersed moans and oaths with boisterous jests. 'There's a good white chest, none of your hairy ones!' he boasted. There was another scene when the doctor arrived. 'What the hell do you want here?' bawled the patient. The doctor withdrew in a hurry and O'Reilly feverishly assured him that the patient was only joking. Finally Collins was examined. The indignity of taking medicine, however, he suffered only when he was alone with O'Reilly.

After a day in bed he announced his intention of getting up. There were several important engagements waiting him. Mrs. MacDonagh and himself quarrelled about it, but when she lost her temper and flung his clothes at him he went meekly back to bed. In despair O'Reilly hid his trousers and went off to beg the Chief of Staff to issue orders that Collins should remain in bed. An order from the Chief of Staff to the Director of Organisations to stay in bed is the only touch of comedy missing from the incident, but the Chief of Staff was a realist. He replied sadly that Collins was not in the least likely to obey orders from him—which was only too true—and O'Reilly went back to find Collins dressed in a blanket while one of his staff went about the house searching distractedly for the missing suit of clothes. When O'Reilly entered, Collins made a grab at him.

'It's my trousers or yours!' he growled.

That evening he went off to an interview at Cullenswood House, walking with an unusually emphatic stride which to all ears spelt out 'I'll show them I can walk'. After that he began to improve, but the pleurisy had left some weakness, because he remained peculiarly susceptible to colds, and another responsibility was added to O'Reilly's lot. He, and he alone, could induce Collins to take medicine, and when a mustard bath—a mustard bath!—was added to this humiliation it was O'Reilly's hands which prepared it, and Collins, twitching his dressing gown about him, glowered and thumped off to the bathroom, speechless with rage.

Already the Collins of the second phase was beginning to take shape: the humorous, vital, tense, impatient figure which shoots through the pages of contemporary history as it shot through the streets of Dublin with a cry of anguish for 'all the hours we waste in sleep'. People were already growing accustomed to his ways; the warning thump of his feet on the stairs as he took them six at a time, the crash of the door and the searching look, and that magnetic power of revivifying the stalest air. People still describe the way in which one became aware of his presence, even when he was not visible, through that uncomfortable magnetism of the very air, a tingling of the nerves. First to wake, he sprang out of bed and stamped about the room as fresh as though he were leaving a cold bath instead of a warm bed. He was peculiarly sensitive to touch and drew away when people tried to paw him. He seemed to be always bundling people out of bed, and not only the long-suffering O'Hegarty and O'Sullivan, who had the doubtful pleasure of sharing a room with him, but all the others, the quiet, simple people who had never thought themselves of use to humanity. Each of his gestures had a purposeful monumental quality; and his face that strange lighting which evaded the photographers but which Doyle-Jones has caught in his bust. One had the impression of a temperament impatient of all restraint, even that imposed from within, exploding in jerky gestures, oaths, jests and laughter; so vital that, like his facial expression, it evades analysis. If I had recorded all the occasions when he wept I should have given the impression that he was hysterical. He wasn't; he laughed and wept as a child does (and indeed, as people in earlier centuries seem to have done) quite without self-consciousness.

Collins' words and actions, considered separately, are commonplace enough; one would need a sort of cinema projector of prose to capture the sense of abounding life they gave to his contemporaries. People who submitted to their influence became intoxicated; work seemed easier, danger slighter, the impossible receded. People who did not were exasperated. 'What insolence!' they cried. 'He doesn't even say good morning.' He said neither good morning nor good night; avoided handshakes as he avoided anything in the least savouring of formality; and when ladies accustomed to good society received him he had time only to ask if anyone was inside, and then brushed past them without a glance.

He knew he was a difficult man; he had no home, no constant refuge, passing from house to house and making demands upon its occupants as he did upon the men who worked for him; yet—though a week rarely passed when one of them, host or colleague, hadn't occasion to complain—there were few who did not serve him cheerfully because of the occasions when a fine and sudden delicacy of feeling showed that he appreciated it. Outsiders, seeing how he worked his courier O'Reilly till the beads of sweat stood out on the lad's face, grew indignant, but suddenly the natural good humour and kindness would break through and he would shout 'Give us a couple of eggs for that melt!' Or it would be someone else's turn—his hostess's, perhaps, whom he would bundle off to bed while he sent O'Reilly for champagne, merely because he thought she had a cold. He was a self-willed man—the consideration often came inopportunely and at random, like a misdirected kiss.

Sometimes it came in the form of champagne, sometimes as a five-pound note, hidden in the linen press. It was the same with the prisoners of his acquaintance. He remembered their little weaknesses, the brand of tobacco or cigarettes they liked. Each week O'Reilly was sent out for the John Cotton tobacco which Austin Stack smoked. Once when Collins' messenger arrived with the daily inquiry for the health of a sick relative tears filled the eyes of Brugha. 'Mick is so kind,' he said brokenly. 'He thinks of everybody.' And Collins was never too busy to write. Small wonder if people turned to him as the man who got things done.

He was not alone in his management of the revolutionary organisation. Harry Boland, too, had escaped, chance having decreed that the two young rascals who had done most to precipitate trouble should be together in escaping it. Boland looked after Sinn Fein, Collins after the Volunteers, and with these two at the top it was most unlikely that moderation would ever show its hideous fangs. The two were thrown more and more together, and their friendship grew into something deeper. They were well matched. They were of the same age, and temperamentally there was an extraordinary kinship between them. They were both pugnacious, both charmers, both touched by the spirit of gasconade. From this until Boland's departure for America they slept, ate, wrestled and hurled together. Observers thought the affection was more on Collins' side than on Boland's. But they were a pleasant pair, a good sight with their magnificent physique, mischievous infantile antics, and abounding good humour, and Boland brought out the convivial side of Collins' character. Boland was the perfect boon companion. He was talkative, and Collins enjoyed the arguments that blew up between them. Beslai gives a description—moving in the light of the subsequent tragedy—of one such argument in which Boland, who was always looking for a fight, wholeheartedly took the pacifist side and Collins that of the soldier. And Mrs. O'Connor remembers another night when they argued in her kitchen until the early hours. Her husband, Batt, had been praising the America of his youth, with its scope and adventurousness. Collins pounced gleefully upon so likely a theme and expanded upon the glories of his London, its good fellowship and freedom, and its theatres—where one saw the drama of the world (he never forgot his love of the theatre). But Boland brought them round with Edwardian Dublin; the trips to the Strawberry Beds and the Dargle Vale, and if it was theatre you wanted, where in the world would you find finer than Saturday night at the Queen's, where the best patriotic melodramas were staged, and the audience hissed the informers and applauded to the echo the Emmets and Tones?

(In the early morning she tiptoed through the house to see that all was well. Their bedroom door, which faced the stairs and hall, was open in case of a surprise; the moonlight fell upon the pillows where the two heads lay, side by side. Collins' bare powerful arm was resting in sleep upon the little table beside two revolvers.)

And so Collins organised his Volunteers, Boland his voters, each with the determination to go as far as the organisations would stand for. How the fight was to be fought neither of them quite knew: the second party to the quarrel had not yet shown his hand. All the plans of the patriots at this time show a curious streak of unreality which represents the transition stage between the romanticism of 1916 and the realism of 1921. They would capture French and hold him as hostage; they would cut off his light and water; they would (and surely no queerer notion came into Collins' teeming brain) remove the Stone of Destiny from the Coronation Chair in Westminster Abbey. Yeats had planned the same thing in the days when he was a member of the Republican Brotherhood, but the notion was better suited to a poet. If the English had really decided to force conscription it is not at all certain what the result would have been. But Ireland, even if it was not actually ready for war, looked ready; and while French anticipated no difficulty, and Henry Wilson reassured Clemenceau, who was beginning to think Lloyd George had cold feet, Lloyd George's cabinet, all but Milner, ratted with amusing vehemence. Within a month it had all blown over; thousands of Collins' raw recruits had gone back to civil life not to be heard of again until the Truce (they hadn't wanted to fight the Germans, but they had no intense desire to come to grips with the English); the English had apparently lost nothing, but in fact they had lost everything—prestige, support, confidence. The Parliamentary Party was utterly discredited. Eighty of them had been unable to break the back of conscription, while a handful of raw country lads with guns in their hands had

55

done it.

No one was more surprised at the victory than Collins; there was scarcely a Republican leader who did not rub his eyes. Now it was their turn. The English had shown they didn't want to fight—the Irish would show they did. Lloyd George had asked French to get the Irish to shoot first. Well, the Irish *would* shoot first.

Some of the Irish, that is. There was still quite a respectable majority of the Sinn Fein Party which looked with the utmost suspicion on Collins and Boland; there was even a large group among the Volunteers who thought the wild young man from Cork was altogether too wild. They showed it at the Sinn Fein convention of October 1918, when again they plumped for safe and reasonable men and left the hotheads and firebrands alone. Collins and Boland raged. It was not that they had not striven to show the delegates the error of their ways. There was the familiar bloc which voted to order, but the delegates continued to look askance at it. The two young bosses decided it would not occur again. Later on, they went carefully through the nominees selected by the local Sinn Fein committees as candidates for the general election and ruthlessly eliminated every man who was likely to cause them trouble. At long last they had the opportunity of establishing an Irish Parliament; the period of waiting was over, and they would see that it would be a fighting parliament. The candidates who did face the electorate when Collins and Boland had finished with the lists were all staunch Republicans; they might be lacking in other graces, but at least they had all proved themselves good haters of compromise. The hotter they talked, the better Collins and Boland liked them. Neither distinguished too carefully between a strong word and a strong blow. These were the men selected to put Griffith's austere policy into effect; it was just as well he was then locked safely away in an English prison or he might have died of an apoplectic fit.

With the electoral ammunition so thoughtfully supplied by the English prime minister, they faced their first general election. It was not so much an election as a rout. The electors were invited to vote for the men who had beaten conscription, and they did. The Parliamentary Party, heavy with sleep and sin, simply disappeared; rarely has any democratic country known such a sweeping up of reactionaries.

But Collins was still in the dark about the future. He attended the funeral of a hunger striker in officer's uniform. It is true that in police headquarters he had Joe Kavanagh, warning him against possible raids, but how easy it would have been to memorise his features! What did he envisage? The most one can say is 'a good fight', and he was a Sinn Feiner only because Arthur Griffith's policy was that which most quickly promised a clash with England. He did not take it seriously; he did not even trouble to understand it. He described it in a monosyllable more vigorous than elegant. Collins was too realistic to attach importance to Griffith's fine points about the Dual Monarchy; the kings, lords and commons of Ireland. But the Sinn Fein cock might be made to fight. The elections gave them the opportunity of putting spurs on the cock.

On the twenty-first of January 1919 Dail Eireann, the assembly of Irish deputies, met for the first time. Collins and Boland were away in England on more urgent business. Huge crowds besieged the Mansion House. There was a big attendance of the world's press; the public rose when the twenty-seven delegates entered. Brugha took the chair; the session was opened by prayer; when the roll was called the clerk answered for most of those absent, 'Imprisoned by the English.'

Only Irish was spoken. The audience listened eagerly, though the majority were unable to understand a word. The Provisional Constitution was read. It provided for a president with a ministry of four. One of the ministries was that of Defence.

The next business was nothing less than a Declaration of Independence, which was read in three languages. Again the people rose. Some were weeping. Whereupon the assembly, having constituted itself a parliament, went on to select delegates to the Peace Conference.

Collins' spirit, if it turned at all to the Mansion House that January day, must have been well pleased. Unless the delegates had actually gone out forthwith and attacked Dublin Castle, they could hardly have been more extreme. Europe, too, was pleased. About the whole proceedings there had been a splendid ceremoniousness which argued well for the determination of the deputies. England professed herself able to laugh at it; Ireland, to her inmost heart, was thrilled. Less than three years, and the Republic which had been stifled in the blood of its founders had been proclaimed anew. Like the little earnest man who presided over it, with the marks of seventeen English bullets in his body, it had risen as though from the dead.

And yet, admitting the magnificence of the gesture, the courage of the challengers, one must ask: was it wise? Was it not an overstatement, both of the intentions of the people and of their actual strength (by strength I mean all the resources, physical and cultural, of a nation)? From this Declaration of Independence, I feel, sprang all the disaster of succeeding years: disunion, anarchy, cultural disintegration. For it one can invoke only one excuse, that, failing such overstatement, the nation would never have risen to the occasion; that the historical process which began at the end of the eighteenth century, and which had turned a people of myths and sagas into something resembling a European nation, could progress only by such violent expansions of spirit, crowding into a few brief years the work of centuries, and, when they burst, plunging the whole nation into a decade of despair and inertia. There had been the illusion of the Protestant nationalists that had died with Emmet, the illusion of the peasantry that had perished in the grass of the roadside or the hold of the coffin ship, the illusion of the townsmen, driven into the cities by the Famine, which had ended in a roadside squabble at Tallaght, there had been the vast illusion of the Parnellite middle classes which the Church had pricked. Did Ireland need yet another illusion before the power of the English ascendancy could be broken? Did that ineluctable historical process require yet another generation of embittered men and women who had known a few years of magnificence and must die with a grudge in their hearts against life for having robbed them of it?

58

No sooner was it made than this Declaration of Independence began to produce its appropriate evils. Up to this the independence movement had been divided roughly into moderates and extremists. Now the extremists were themselves being divided into those like Collins, who took the declaration for what it was worth, the largest standard on the highest mast, and those like Brugha, who took it for what it said. Though Brugha had never liked Collins' secret organisation he had been glad enough to see it used against Griffith and the moderates. Now with his loyalty to his oath, to the state which he had created, and to the government of which he was a member, he would tend more and more to look jealously at this Brotherhood, which had a different oath, and which looked upon its own Supreme Council as the real government of Ireland.

Both Brugha and Collins were pleased, and only Griffith and the moderates were horrified when on the selfsame day Breen, of Tipperary, in seizing some gelignite, had occasion to kill two armed policemen. It was an ironic commentary upon the solemn ceremony in the Mansion House and on Lloyd George's instructions to French. The ice was broken, the first shots, as Lloyd George desired, had been fired by the rebels, and Arthur Griffith, on the very day when his policy triumphed over those of all his enemies, might bid a long goodbye to his dream that from it would spring the ordered, peaceful reconstruction of a nation.

CHAPTER VI

ON THE RUN

THE possibility of de Valera's escape from Lincoln had been suggested, and Collins took it up with his usual enthusiasm. With the aid of an altar candle de Valera had succeeded in getting an impression of the chaplain's key. A drawing of it was sent out. Collins had a key made and smuggled in. It was a failure. A fresh copy was made, and this, too, was wrong. One of the prisoners then made a key of stuff sent in by Collins, and the escape was fixed for the night of the third of February. The plan was that Collins and Boland should superintend the actual escape, place de Valera and his fellow jail breakers in a car which would take them to Worksop, where Fintan Murphy would be waiting with another car. Murphy would send them on to the next control station at Sheffield, and so the prisoners would be passed from hand to hand until they reached a safe hiding place in Manchester. Collins' inspected every detail down to the testing of the rope ladder which he had brought from Ireland.

On the night fixed, the two friends, Collins and Boland, were in waiting outside the jail. They showed a light. De Valera replied, and he and his two companions began to make their way through the grounds to the side gate by which they hoped to escape. Outside this was an iron gate which had not figured in the reckoning. Collins tried his own key in it. To his horror it broke as de Valera, MacGarry and Milroy opened the door on the other side. Collins groaned his consternation. De Valera thrust his own key into the stuffed lock, the broken key fell out at Collins' feet, and the three prisoners were free. Collins and Boland saw them into the waiting car and went off in high glee to celebrate.

It was the beginning of an extraordinary development in Collins' organisation, by which, through hundreds of individual contacts, he gradually reached the point at which he knew everything that happened to prisoners, and even when the job of freeing them proved impossible he could give their gaolers the uneasy feeling that everything they did was observed. There was nothing out of the ordinary about this except the almost meticulous organisation in which there was no one too humble to be of use, and no detail too trifling not to add to the general picture. Collins' genius was entirely one of detail.

To counter the effect of this escape the English authorities decided upon a general release, implying that they had actually connived at it. De Valera, who had been talking of going to America, was now free to return to Dublin, and his lieutenants pressed him to do so. On the twenty-second of March 1919, a statement, signed by the two acting secretaries of Sinn Fein, one of whom was Boland, announced that he would be received with national rejoicing, that a procession would meet him at the gates of the city and escort him to the Mansion House, where he would deliver a message to the Irish people.

This was pretty strong. The Castle, foaming at the mouth, replied by prohibiting the reception. A meeting of the Sinn Fein executive was held to consider what should be done. Figgis, who was enraged that Collins had secured the elimination of his candidature at the general election, asked for the authority of the secretaries. Apparently the second secretary had not even known of it, much less subscribed his name. It was another Collins–Boland plot to involve respectable men in trouble. Collins instantly jumped up and accepted responsibility. He had written the announcement of the reception, and he didn't care who knew it. The Volunteers were the proper authorities for such a measure. They wanted fighting and the sooner fighting came the better. And they wanted no 'cowards'.

There was no mistake about it, this was the Big Fellow of Stafford and Frongoch once again. He thrust out his chin, tossed his head, frowned, spat out his hatred and contempt for the moderates just as he had done in the old days. It was quite plain, he did not give a damn for any political organisation which did not subserve the interests of the fighting men. It was just cheek on their part, setting up to dictate policy to their youngers and betters. This was too much for Arthur Griffith. This young man had coolly thrust him out of tne presidency of his own organisation and honeycombed it with Volunteers and secret-society men; he had made it elect fourscore dyed-in-the wool Republicans as its parliamentary representatives, to the exclusion of his own personal friends and associates like Figgis; had made that supposed Sinn Fein Parliament, some of whose members had never even read the Sinn Fein constitution, declare an Irish Republic instead of a Dual Monarchy; and

61

now had the impudence to stand up and maintain that even the shadow of a democratic organisation which was left had no right to an opinion of its own. Griffith rose, a picture of outraged majesty, and thundered forth the democratic doctrine : that meeting, and that meeting alone, had the right to decide.

After a furious battle of words, a truce was declared to secure de Valera's opinion—de Valera, of course, had not even been consulted—and de Valera, who had come disappointingly moderate ever since his election to the presidency, ordered the abandonment of the reception. For the present the young diehards had to postpone their free fight with the British; they were bitterly disappointed, for the idea of open fighting died hard in their minds, and the 'murder campaign', as the British called the sort of fighting which afterwards took place, was the very last thing they foresaw or desired.

While preparing the blow, which did not come off, Collins had carried out another piece of jail breaking. This time it was Robert Barton. For Barton Collins entertained a very high regard. He was a Wicklow landowner, who, as an English Officer, had been so impressed by the ideals and behaviour of his prisoners during the Rising of 1916 that he had joined them and found himself in turn an officer of the rebel army, a member of the Republican Parliament, and finally a prisoner himself. Collins admired him because, always studious, he was attracted by anyone possessing qualities he lacked. Barton was one of a succession of people of his class whom Collins, the man of feeling, admired; such were Childers and his wife, the Davies, Douglas, Cope, the Laverys, Birkenhead. The escapes he organised were always with a definite purpose. He needed Barton's financial head and knowledge of the world. So Barton must be rescued. He succeeded in smuggling him in a file and rope, and probably with conscious mischief, arranged with Mrs. O'Connor to prepare a room for him. One Sunday evening in spring, while a bright moon was shining and pious Dublin was at its devotions, Barton, who had sawn through a bar in his cell window and made a dummy in case any warder should come peeping through the cell door, got out. Collins' men were waiting outside, and at Barton's signal they threw over a rope ladder; he climbed the wall, and they caught him in an outstretched blanket. When Mrs. O'Connor saw him she recognised the English officer who had been so courteous to her during her husband's imprisonment three years before.

The next man Collins wanted out was Fleming. Fleming had shown a perfect genius for obstreperousness, and Collins felt he would be simply invaluable. The jailers had done their damnedest to break his spirit and failed. No handcuffs made could defeat him, he worked free of them all; refused to wear prison clothes, lay naked, smashed everything he could lay his hands on, until he had made an utter wreck of his cell, and finally beat the authorities into admitting defeat. This was the sort of man to warm the cockles of Collins' heart; he adored spirit.

On the twenty-ninth of March 1919 a small group of men were standing on the canal bank outside Mountjoy Prison. With them was O'Reilly with three bicycles. At a signal from within they threw a rope ladder over the wall. A head appeared; it was Beaslai's. O'Reilly's instructions from Collins were to see that whoever did not escape, Fleming did. O'Reilly shouted to Beaslai, and Beaslai replied that Fleming was coming. Before O'Reilly left to report to Collins close upon twenty prisoners had come over the wall.

Collins was waiting in the lounge of the Wicklow Hotel for news. O'Reilly, having deposited his precious charge in safe keeping, arrived to report. Collins' first query was 'Is Fleming out?'

'The whole jail is out,' cried O'Reilly.

'What?' asked Collins. 'How many?'

'About twenty when I came away.'

Collins looked at him in stupefaction and then burst into a wild guffaw of delight. He crammed on his hat and rushed for the door to interview Fleming. While he worked at Cullenswood House that evening O'Reilly noticed how frequently he laid down his pen and burst into a shrill chuckle. It was a trick of his whenever something tickled his imagination, and O'Reilly knew he was picturing the consternation of the governor when he arrived to find his prison practically empty.

It was as though the Volunteers were testing themselves on battles for prestige, leaving the bloodier trials for later. As yet they were only pulling faces and tweaking noses.

A few days later Dail Eireann met for the second time. De Valera was elected President, and as his cabinet he chose Collins (Finance), Griffith, Brugha, Plunkett, Cosgrave, Mac-Neil, Barton and Countess Markievicz. It was a delicate bit of balancing to satisfy both moderates and extremists.

The patriots had now pledged themselves to go on with all the regular business of government. They would create a state within a state, a complete set of departments, with a permanent civil service and a regular army. Many of those departments never functioned, some perhaps were never intended to function, and to an unprejudiced eye it is clear that such a challenge risked the whole future of the movement. Failure could result in nothing but ridicule; for the Parliamentarians were hovering still upon the outskirts of the nation, though their derisive shouts of 'rainbow chasers' were growing fainter.

It is characteristic of Collins that from the beginning he does not seem to have thought at all of the impossibilities latent in the scheme; to him it meant exactly what it said, and he tolerated none of the slackness that could, and did, so easily arise from its inherent fantasticalness. He was a born improvisator, and from the moment he was appointed Minister of Finance the Department of Finance began to function; within a few weeks his mighty loan was under way, and even today, when we have forgotten, or can no longer imagine, the preposterous conditions under which the Department worked—censorship, imprisonment, confiscation, murder—one is filled with respect for the variety and thoroughness of the work performed. That is more than can be said for most of the other departments. 'Stack,' hissed Collins to a cabinet colleague later on, 'your department is only a —— joke.'

From this until the end of the struggle some of the departments were, as Collins described Austin Stack's, 'only a —— joke.'

'It seems,' wrote Collins of one of them, 'that the department works in continuous fear of a raid. Nobody ever seems to be there, and generally speaking, the Accountant General finds it impossible to get his work done in time.' But the Ministers had other things to consider. One of them, writing to the Director of Publicity, makes the important suggestion that 'pillar stones should be erected in suitable positions in New York, Paris and Rome, upon which should be inscribed from day to day the names of "convicted rebels" executed by the British. A great deal of propaganda could be done from Moscow in collaboration with the Turks, Egyptians, Indians, Persians and Russians.'

Hunted from pillar to post, Collins studied banking and economics. Nor was it ever a mere pedestrian efficiency. He, like all the young men about him, was filled with a sense of deep responsibility, a high idealism which embraced all the forms of life, music, literature and art. One of the first steps of the new government was to provide from their small resources a fund for Irish scholarship. The money was used to finance the publication of Thurneysen's classical work on the Irish sagas.

Of the other appointments, the most interesting, as it was the most momentous, is that of Brugha as Minister of Defence. When proposing for ministers a higher salary than that contemplated, Brugha made the highly significant announcement that he did not propose to draw his own but to hand it over to his Chief of Staff, Mulcahy. This should have been warning enough to anybody that Brugha's acceptance of office would be little more than nominal. With it began the cleavage between Brugha and Collins, and the throwing upon the shoulders of anyone prepared to carry it of the enormous responsibility of an untrained citizen army which, almost unknown to itself, was being drawn into conflict with a mighty empire.

From this until John Devoy spoke of Collins as 'Commander-in-Chief of the Irish army', Brugha was fast asleep to the realities of the situation. His methods were always clear and simple. On one occasion he was followed by a spy. He turned and the spy turned; in a moment it was he who was following the spy. The spy ran and Brugha ran. The chase, growing hotter, continued into a public park, where the spy took refuge in a lavatory. When Brugha broke down the door the spy escaped through the roof.

He worked on in his office on the quays. He had no escape there. He had no intention of escaping from anyone. Plain Cathal Brugha, riddled with bullets, had refused to escape in 1916. The Minister for Defence of the Irish Republic would certainly not show his heels. If the soldiers came a bell would ring downstairs, and Brugha would meet them on the stairhead with his Peter the Painter.

The Minister of Defence did not die heroically on the candlemaker's stair for the simple reason that the distracted officers from the country, seeking advice and assistance, came to his younger and more energetic colleague, who might be seen anywhere on any day of the week. Collins received them with outstretched hand and a 'How's Paddy?' or, for the matter of that, a growl and a 'What the bloody hell do you want now?' which they liked almost as well.

Meanwhile he was showing himself only too ready to eat up the work that others neglected. He was beginning to form that considerable and important organisation of the ports, through which wanted men passed out and wanted arms passed in. A little group of his old friends in England provided the con-tacts. Sailors were sworn into the secret organisation, and soon each of them was carrying dispatches or arms; every morning O'Reilly met the incoming boat at the North Wall and the 'Irish Mail', as the secret channel was called, was in motion. Gelignite from the Welsh coal fields, packed in tin trunks, rifles in baskets marked 'China—Fragile' or in sections in sailors' bags, revolvers and equipment stowed anyhow, were smuggled ashore each morning under the eyes of police and detectives.

It has already been mentioned that Colliins had got into touch with Joe Kavanagh and Broy. Broy was on duty at detective headquarters in Brunswick Street. While Dail Eireann was sitting, Collins carried out one of his most daring coups. Late at night Broy brought him into headquarters. Up

They searched it from floor to ceiling, followed by O'Reilly, whom at one stage they arrested as being 'Collins' man' and released only at the request of the Lord Mayor. At one moment they actually stood in the yard, looking up at the missing panes of glass, and Collins and his companions heard them discuss the possibility of anyone's getting through them. After close on three hours they departed, and Collins came down, covered in dust. He had found himself in a contractor's store and busied himself with preparations for dropping into the yard of an adjoining garage.

Meanwhile the Mansion House was filling with guests for the public reception of the American delegates, though everything was in disorder; no carpets down, and flowers and seats missing. Collins was filthy. While he washed he sent O'Reilly home for his uniform and, when the reception was actually in progress, created a sensation by appearing in it: the wanted man, and the only officer in uniform in that large and gay assembly.

Collins was still showing off.

CHAPTER VII

WAR

COLLINS was disappointed in de Valera. No sooner was he out of prison than he announced his intention of going to America. In America Collins had never more than a minor interest. With his realist's passion for the immediate task he felt de Valera's place was at home. A year later he hit off his attitude in a phrase addressed to one of the Irish representatives abroad. 'Our propaganda can never be stronger than our actions at home.' Of America he asked men and arms. After a certain trying experience he reduced it to one for arms only.

Not that de Valera was much use except as a symbol of

resistance. He was an austere and earnest leader who gave dignity to the whole movement, but he had never proved himself an administrator. Again and again his meticulousness got on Collins' nerves, for Collins had one of those queer lightning minds which never halt before a word or a decision. De Valera fidgeted and brooded over every sentence like a hen on an egg. While they were preparing Ireland's case for the Peace Conference, Collins was in a fever of impatience. 'The damned Peace Conference will be over before he's satisfied,' was his comment. And a Press statement of a few hundred words cost de Valera just the same anguish. He could not bear to part from it until he had weighed every word to the thousandth part of a grain of sense. 'I never met such a bloody man,' said Collins to Desmond Ryan when de Valera withheld an unimportant interview.

But de Valera had his way. In April 1919 Boland went across to prepare his reception. Collins and his other friends celebrated it with an American wake.

One Friday evening at the end of May Steve Lanigan met Dick O'Neill and Barney Downes in Liverpool. All three were Collins' men. Downes was bos'n on the *Lapland*. He was signing on a crew and asked Lanigan if there was any refugee waiting to be shipped. Lanigan said no and went off with O'Neill to a near-by pub to find a long dispatch from Collins waiting him. There was an unusual emphasis about the form. 'I am writing you on a most important matter, and one that may be very, very urgent. We have decided here that the time is just about ripe for Dev. to get away to America, and we are therefore putting the arrangements in your hands.' There followed the usual minute instructions about de Valera's seaman's book, and a warning that he must not be brought over from Ireland until arrangements were complete—a necessary one as events showed.

Lanigan sent O'Neill to warn Downes and later sent him by boat to Dublin to bring de Valera back. It was Sunday morning before O'Neill saw Collins. They both went straight to Greystones to interview de Valera. Collins had no difficulty in persuading the President to take advantage of the opportunity,

70

and on Sunday night he and O'Neill crossed together. He was recognised by many of the passengers, including the priest who had attended him in 1916. At Chester the detectives were already on his track, and O'Neill made him transfer to the Great Western Line. When they alighted at Birkenhead they were still watched. They then crossed the Mersey and took a taxi to Lanigan's house. Lanigan was not there, because he and Hurley had been waiting at Edgehill Station. When they returned at 3 a.m. de Valera was waiting for them. At six de Valera put on a black scarf with his blue suit, dragged an old cap over his eyes, and set out with O'Neill on a workman's tram.

'Here,' said O'Neill, 'carry me bag!' and the President of the newborn Irish Republic strode through the docks on his way to a more than royal New York reception and an isolation in its own way more complete than any prison.

He left Collins to an uncomfortable dual existence as fantastic as any which could be imagined. Collins was naturally a great businessman, and he shouldered his responsibilities in a thoroughly businesslike way. This energetic man, who kept a file for every transaction, who insisted on supervising every detail and went nowhere without his secretary, bore very little resemblance to the Collins of legend and none at all to the revolutionary of fiction. Beside him, Lenin, with his theories, feuds and excommunications, seems a child, and not a particularly intelligent one. He ran the whole Revolution as though it were a great business concern, ignoring all the rules. In his files can be found receipts for the lodging of political refugees side by side with those for sweeping brushes and floor polish. He might be seen a dozen times a day in shops, offices, restaurants, pubs, with solicitors, clergymen, bankers, intellectuals. He permitted no restriction on his freedom and cycled unguarded about the city as though the British Empire had never existed. In the evenings he might be seen at the Abbey Theatre, tossing restlessly in his seat, or in the summer at a race meeting, rubbing shoulders with British officers and Secret-Service men.

The other Collins, the romantic figure, 'which this person

was certainly not', as his enemy Brugha said with the clarity of hate, and who has become by far the more widely known, was merely incidental; the real Collins, sitting at his desk, signing correspondence, found the necessity for the romantic figure's existence a mere disturbance of routine. Collins, of course, had the romantic streak, the power of self-dramatisation, which went with his daemonic temperament, but that is a different kettle of fish; his genius was the genius of realism. Answering a business letter in a businesslike way, he would be made aware of the English garrison as a sort of minor interruption and hit out at it as a busy man hits out at a bluebottle.

For the moment the bluebottle took the form of the English police system, which interrupted his work by raiding his offices and imprisoning his staffs: he proceeded grimly to get rid of it. As we know, he was in touch with Kavanagh and Broy over the head of the nominal Director of Intelligence (he was always blandly indifferent to what constituted another's preserves), and these, at great peril, kept him informed of pending raids and arrests. He now had himself appointed Director of Intelligence and began to organise his new department on the same thorough businesslike lines. Tobin, with whom he had discussed taking the Stone of Destiny, he made his lieutenant. Tobin was a young man who had shown talent for the sort of intelligence work that appealed to Collins: the collecting and filing of all the apparently inessential data. Tobin gathered together a small staff which later included Cullen and Thornton, took an office in Crow Street, and began to accumulate from such unexceptionable sources as 'Who's Who' and the *Morning Post* information regarding the movements, present and past, the appearance, hobbies and social connections of everyone connected with British government in Ireland. He also selected a group of daring spirits to carry out the work which the director planned—the Squad. These were whole-time employees who went about the city armed or with guns convenient, ready to pounce when Collins gave the word. It was a typical piece of Collins' organisation, this office within a stone's throw of the Castle gate, and might take pride of place in the *Handbook for Revolutionists* which he should have

72

written. Once more, against the rules of the game, which prescribed furtiveness, disguises, absence of documents—all the tricks of the popular novelists which have been resorted to by revolutionists in the past—Collins brazenly asserted his absolute right to unrestricted freedom of movement and the most thorough pedestrian efficiency; his assistants all but punched their tickets in a time clock. On this modest and inexpensive organisation he proceeded to build up for himself a name of fear such as no Irish leader had ever enjoyed.

Each of his contacts, like each of his departments, was kept in a watertight receptacle. Tobin and the others were informed of the agents whom they were required to meet and no more. Unknown to them, Collins held a weekly conference with Broy and Kavanagh at Gay's house in Clontarf. A third detective now made his appearance. Kavanagh thought highly of him, though among the Castle officials he was looked upon as their most reliable man. He was one of a loyalist family; young, daring, resolute and a crack shot. Kavanagh took him for long walks, dropping casual cautious remarks about the disturbed state of the country and reporting to Collins the replies young MacNamara made. It is one of those situations dear to the heart of the novelist with which the period abounds. When MacNamara was introduced he took Collins by storm. Within a year Joe Kavanagh had died, but he had left a man to fill his place.

It was a curious conference: Collins, the high-powered young organiser, whose name was already gathering light and magic; Kavanagh; MacNamara; Broy. They had tea and pancakes and talked athletics before settling down to work. Carbon copies of secret documents were produced, which they discussed, or group photographs of the detective division which found their way into Tobin's omnivorous filing system. Sometimes these conferences resulted in startling discoveries, as when a document was produced concerning American sailors which caused the British government unholy embarrassment at Washington.

Collins had succeeded, as no Irish leader before him had done, in thrusting his foot firmly against the half-open gate of

Dublin Castle, and England would find it impossible to shut it again.

The first victim of the new Intelligence Service was Detective-Sergeant Smith, known as the 'Dog Smith', the Uriah Heep of the force. In July 1919, after several warnings, he was shot down outside his own house in Drumcondra.

It was Collins' first killing. Then, as afterwards, he did everything to avoid the necessity for it. With his strange sensitiveness he was haunted for days before by the thought of it. He was morose and silent. When the day of the shooting came, people saw for the first time the curious tension which was repeated over and over again in the years to come. The same scene occurred so often that it became familiar. O'Reilly was usually in waiting somewhere near to bring back a report. As he faltered out the words in answer to the quick glance of his chief, Collins began to stride up and down the room, swinging his arms in wide half circles and grinding his heels into the floor. For ten or fifteen minutes he continued this in silence; then he grabbed a paper and tried to read. But his eyes strayed from the printed columns to the window with an empty, faraway look. Then, raging, he turned upon the unoffending O'Reilly.

But what of Griffith, who had been left behind to take de Valera's place? What of that most galling of moderates, with his Dual Monarchy? How did he react to the shootings, which he must have known to be the work of Collins? Griffith, too, was answering to his responsibilities. The men of peace, the moderates, who had been pushed aside by Collins, found a new Griffith who showed himself strongly averse to using his authority to restrain Collins. One quality Griffith had developed beyond all others, that of loyalty. He had always maintained he was no leader; he was showing now that he could be a good follower. Under Griffith the fighting men had a liberty which they could never have had under their chosen leader.

Meanwhile Collins went ahead, with his customary thoroughness, organising the National Loan. It was not made easier by the British who grew alarmed and set themselves to suppress it from the start. They suppressed the newspapers which published its advertisements. The printing had to be done secretly, meetings held secretly, literature and receipts kept hidden from police and military raids. An enormous mass of correspondence had to be dealt with in the same underhand way, money had to be carried by messengers; and every obstacle provided a reasonable excuse for inefficiency. 'If you saw some of the particulars we were supplied with,' he wrote, 'they would simply drive you mad.'

It is no job for an easygoing man, and Collins cracked the whip. Many men in country parishes remember him only as organiser of the Loan; and how they trembled before him. Alibis were vain; he knew the capacity of every townland.

The organisation of the Volunteers gave him the excuse for a visit home, his last until the Truce. A Volunteer camp had been started in Glandore under the guise of a summer school for Irish. MacKee and Collins intended it for the training of officers—a preliminary to the flying columns. Collins stopped on his way down to visit his brother. It was harvest-time and he worked in the fields, stooking the corn with Sean.

He had a great night at the local pub, where the neighbours came from far and near to see him. He paid for a half tierce of the local beer—Clonakilty Wrashler—and hoisted it single-handed on to the counter; Joe O'Reilly sang a number of his favourite come-all-ye's, while Collins, swinging his heels on the counter, beat time with head and fist.

With more than the usual fire he recited his own particular party piece, 'The List'.

> 'So here's to the Maine and we're sorry for Spain,
> Said Kelly and Burke and Shea.

Then, sitting on a barrel with the old neighbours, he went back upon the tales of the abortive rising of '67, of Scully, the Fenian Head Centre, who had escaped by boat, and the brave old boatman whose four sons had escorted him, and who, awaiting the arrival of the trackers, stove in thirty-three fine boats along the strand, as well as the first policeman.

Even at this distance of years one can fondly imagine that group, loud with liquor and love, making their way home through the summer darkness by dim laneways, their voices coming fainter and fainter to Collins' ears—his people, his passion, his faith.

PART TWO

THE BODY AND THE LASH

CHAPTER VIII

SPIES

THE year 1919 which had begun so lightly and with such little apprehension of what it had in store was drawing to a sanguinary close. The blood of the Volunteers was up. Tired of being harassed and hunted, deported and beaten up, they began to turn upon their pursuers and hit out at soldiers, police and spies as circumstances permitted and with whatever weapons they found handy.

On the twelfth of September 1919 Collins had a narrow shave at 6 Harcourt Street and escaped by dodging police and soldiers from room to room while his colleagues were arrested. Dan Hoey, the pious detective, who had betrayed MacDermott in 1916 and hoped to do the same by Collins, died next day as he stood outside police headquarters in Brunswick Street.

For some time Collins had been planning the escape of Stack and Beaslai from Manchester Prison. He had even visited Stack. In late October, with the aid of Collins' friends from Manchester and Liverpool, these, with four other prisoners, got away and were smuggled by 'Irish Mail' to Dublin. Stack was suffering from a septic leg, which had been made worse by being torn in his climb over the prison wall, and for the long weeks he was detained in Batt O'Connor's, Collins visited him each day, as, a few months before, he had visited Neil Kerr.

On the very day of the prisoners' arrival he had another narrow shave. The new house which he had bought in Harcourt Street, after the capture of No. 6, was raided. He had prepared for an escape by having a light ladder made which he pulled up after him as he emerged through the skylight. He crawled across the roofs until he reached the skylight of the

Standard Hotel. Here he had also arranged to have the sky-light permanently open and a light ladder in readiness; but the ladder was missing, and to his horror, as he hastily swung himself down, he saw beneath him not the landing but the well of the staircase. Swinging from the ledge of the window, he leaped with sufficient energy to clear the rail of the landing but hurt himself badly in the fall. Meanwhile the Squad had been summoned. They were posted at points of vantage about the raiders, waiting for Collins to be dragged out. They got a shock when they saw him emerge from the Standard Hotel with a wide grin on his face and drive off on a hackney car laughing at their bewilderment.

It was possible the 76 Harcourt Street had been given away by one of a small group who should never have been allowed to know of its existence. Half an hour before the raid one of these had been turned from the door by O'Reilly and informed that Collins was in the country. He went away grumbling. Naturally, he fell under suspicion. His name was Quinlisk. Earlier in the year he had arrived in Dublin in English uniform—a tall, well-built man with cadaverous features. He had served with Casement's Brigade in Germany and, stranded there after the Armistice, gone through the Civil War. He was a vain man, comparatively well educated for his rank, and took occasion to inform Collins that he spoke German fluently. Collins, under the impression that he might prove useful as a training officer, got him a suit of clothes and accommodation at his own lodgings and, even for some time after it became clear that Corporal Quinlisk was of no earthly use to the Volunteers, gave him money. Quinlisk soon proved himself not only no object of charity but a confounded nuisance. He and an associate haunted Collins' office and were incensed when he refused to see any more of them. Yet when he fell seriously ill, Collins once more unloosed the purse strings.

Some time later members of parliament were astonished to receive a visit from Quinlisk. He came to complain of the scandalous way he had been treated by Collins, and announced that he proposed to leave for America to complain of him to John Devoy!

Quinlisk's behaviour is an interesting example of the informer's type of mind, so compact of treachery that it is rarely content with deceiving one side and ultimately deceives only itself; the analogy of insanity is so close that it cannot be overlooked. His imaginary grievance against Collins was the way in which he prepared himself to earn the reward for his capture. When he did offer to betray Collins one may be quite certain he had taught himself to hate him so much that he was utterly unconscious of treachery. On the eleventh of November 1919 he wrote to the Under Secretary, Dublin Castle, stating that he had been connected with Sinn Fein and was now prepared to tell all he knew of it.

'The scoundrel, Michael Collins, has treated me scurvily,' he wrote, 'and now I am going to wash my hands of the whole business. If you accept my offer then please send a man, one who can be trusted, to the above address on tomorrow evening at four o'clock.'*

Dublin Castle jumped at the offer; for some reason informers were scarce, and Quinlisk was interviewed. The notes of the interview were immediately in Collins' hands.

Quinlisk now approached Collins again with the story that he had merely gone to police headquarters about his passport to America (that this idea had been in his mind we already know; it was associated with Collins, and it was an explanation natural and satisfying to himself). What had actually happened, of course, is that after the fateful interview at Dublin Castle his conscience had begun to prick him, and he was deceiving himself into the belief that he was really helping Collins, pretending to accept Quinlisk's account of his interview, determined to trap one of the police superintendents. Disguising his voice, Cullen rang him up, pretended to be Quinlisk, and asked the Superintendent to call at his house in Eccles Street. The Superintendent suggested an interview in Parliament Street. The Squad was in waiting. The group of policemen came as far as the top of Parliament Street, but, except for one of Collins' men acting as a decoy, the rain-

* Quoted in Beaslai: *Michael Collins and the Making of a New Ireland*.

lashed street was empty, and the policemen, becoming suspicious, withdrew. Quinlisk was later accused of trying to double-cross them. The informer was naturally dumbfounded but seems to have realised Collins' intention and played up to it. Quinlisk wrote to a friend of Collins describing this interview.

'He then asked me if I was prepared to close with his offer and endeavour to find out where Collins was stopping, for, said he, where he is the others are too. He said further that the next business would be on a large scale. I asked him what he meant, and he said if he had to search every house in Dublin he would do it. He made no mention this time of swearing falsely against any one. It's a pity I can't get two trustworthy men, and I'd invite the boys to come to 48 (this was Quinlisk's residence), and we'd finish him off.'*

Quinlisk's conscience must have jumped in a lamentable way, because, not content with this, he wrote to the *Freeman's Journal*, giving his own highly coloured account of Dublin Castle's attempt to bribe him, written in a tone of scandalised virtue. The letter, while no doubt quite correct in the information it provides, when read side by side with Quinlisk's original letter offering to betray Collins, gives an astonishing picture of a mind entirely obscured by its own capacity for self-deception.

'At last he [O'Brien] asked me if I had been mixed up with Sinn Fein long, and if I knew anything about those men who were committing the police murders. I replied evasively, and he said, "Sinn Fein has let you down, now it's up to you to get your own back; you will benefit materially and will also be doing good for your country." He then questioned me as to the possibility of Mr. Michael Collins, M.P., staying at the Munster Hotel [the lodgings which Collins had actually shared with Quinlisk] or Vaughan's, and whether I could advise him as to what time he should raid any place where Collins would be likely to stay.... At the latter end of November I received a note from Superintendent O'Brien, inviting me to come to the Castle. I went and was shown into

* Quoted in Beaslai, op. cit.

82

his office at the Lower Yard. He asked me if I had succeeded in locating Collins, and told me that Colonel Johnstone was prepared to give me £50 if Collins were arrested, and a much larger sum of money if I would swear that I had seen Mr. C. interviewing certain men and giving money and instructions to those men before raids were carried out or policemen shot. . . . On Tuesday evening, the ninth of this month, I was again summoned to the Castle, where Superintendent O'Brien asked me if I could give him any information regarding the plans for a guerilla warfare, which was to be carried out by the Volunteers on the following day or Thursday. . . . In giving this account of how Dublin Castle endeavours to do their nefarious work in Ireland, I am actuated only by the desire to open the eyes of our own people and of the English. That Mr. O'Brien should calmly suggest to me that I swear falsely against my own countrymen, and be rewarded by immunity and monetarily, shows what respect these very people have for the law, which it is their duty to uphold and maintain.'*

This is the style of a man in a blue funk about what he has done. The supposed infamous suggestions of O'Brien sound far more like the actual information Quinlisk had given and which with a despairing twist of the mind he is now fathering on to someone else. Unfortunately for him, this letter, violent enough to have committed him to a safe course of action, was not published, and his cupidity was tempted by the increased reward of £10,000 offered on the twenty-fifth of January 1920, immediately after the shooting of Redmond. Ten thousand pounds was big money, and the poor wretch determined to earn it. He made various attempts to discover Collins' whereabouts. Fleming, one of those he came to, informed Collins, and Collins sprang a favourite trap of his. Fleming was instructed to tell Quinlisk that Collins was staying at his native place in Clonakilty. Immediately after, Collins intercepted this valuable piece of information on its way south. Quinlisk, apparently terrified lest anyone else should claim the reward, bolted after it. He went to Clonakilty but, finding that Collins was not there, flew into a panic. He wrote two letters

* Quoted in Beaslai, op. cit.

to Fleming demanding Collins' whereabouts and followed this up with a wire for funds!

In Cork he began again upon his old tricks and offered to buy arms for the Volunteers. They kept their eye on him from a distance. One night they decoded a wire addressed to the local inspector. It merely stated that a dispatch of great importance had been forwarded that night. Next day they held up the policeman carrying the mail and found that the dispatch dealt with Quinlisk, who was recommended to the inspector as a Secret Service agent from headquarters. They arrested Quinlisk, who had in his possession a letter from the assistant police intelligence officer in Dublin warning him that he was undertaking the trip to Cork at his own risk. They sent a messenger to Collins for permission to shoot him, and that evening the permission came by wire.

On the eighteenth of February 1920 he met the usual fate of spies on a lonely road outside the city. He is a rather pathetic figure with his grievance, his treachery, his funk, his loquacity and his conceit, one of those figures which move in a sort of perpetual twilight of the mind, like the shadows of real men.

At the same time that Dublin Castle was trying to trap Collins with the aid of Quinlisk, it was using other and far more effective methods.

In November there arrived in Dublin a small plump gentleman wearing knee breeches and boots laced up his calves. He had sharp features and a plausible air. He took a room in the Granville Hotel, giving a vague hint that he was agent for a firm dealing in musical instruments; he was affable though not gregarious, dined alone, and found recreation in the works of Edgar Wallace. Among the staff of the hotel he let it be understood that a portion of his youth had been spent in the wild West, and jokingly declared his preference for it. There, he said, they did not shoot you but tied you to a wild pony and lashed it off, giving you some chance of life. In the mornings he wrote a good deal—business letters no doubt—but sometimes he went out to Fairview—birdcatching, of all strange amusements. He had a passion for birds, and there were usually three or four cages in his bedroom.

One must give Mr. Jameson credit for a real if macabre sense of humour, though perhaps he underestimated the elusiveness of the birds he was now trying to lime. For, in his time, Mr. Jameson had caught many more things than birds. His real name was Burn, and he was the son of a Limerick police inspector; though his acquaintance with Ireland was slight, he was clever enough to conceal it. He was a smart Secret Service Man, an ex-soldier, who had seen service in India and Germany; after a spell in London, during which he represented himself as an ardent Communist and acted as *agent provocateur* in the police strike, he got into touch with the Irish Self-Determination League. Its secretary, Art O'Brien, furnished him with an introduction to Collins.

So far, luck had favoured Mr. Jameson. It was to favour him so much more that its desertion of him would be one of the minor tragedies of circumstance: an incredible tangle of coincidence which would make a story of Thomas Hardy's look tame. Certainly, he was fortune's fool.

O'Reilly, Collins' messenger, who received him, was the first to take alarm. He reported that the man was an obvious cheat. Collins merely growled and sent him off with a fistful of letters; summonses to General Headquarters Staff to meet their new friend at Mrs. O'Keeffe's restaurant in Camden Street. Tobin and Cullen, warned by O'Reilly, did not put in an appearance. But the rest did, and Mr. Jameson explained his modest mission. He was a representative of the Russian government, which was anxious to avenge itself for the interventionist policy of Churchill by organising mutinies in the British army. He had already agents in every military barracks who would assist the Irish with arms and equipment. He also pretended he had contacts with the Birmingham Small Arms Factory. At the word 'arms' headquarters cocked its ears. It liked Mr. Jameson so much that it arranged for a further meeting, which duly took place over tea in Mrs. O'Kelly's house in Ranelagh.

But Tobin and Cullen were not allowed to escape so easily. Collins had not yet seen the miracle man and proposed to do so at Batt O'Connor's, where he lunched each day with Austin

Stack. So the two disgusted lieutenants picked up Mr. Jameson and brought him out on the Donnybrook tram. Mrs. O'Connor, when she opened the door and saw the plump face and sharp features of Mr. Jameson, also took fright. She drew Cullen aside and asked him who the visitor was. Cullen threw up his hands in despair. Collins was as obstinate as a mule. He also liked Mr. Jameson, and another interview was arranged for the following day.

Now fortune began to realise the really scurvy trick she could play on her apparent favourite as, full of glee, he rushed off from Brendan Road to arrange for the capture of the notorious Collins, the man who had outwitted the whole detective force of Dublin and who had fallen into his hands like a ripe apple.

There was at this time a new assistant commissioner of police reorganising the Detective Division in Dublin Castle. He was Redmond, from Belfast, a stocky fellow, energetic, very clever, and not unkind. He began with a pardonable distrust of his force, which he proposed to purify and strengthen with Belfast Orangemen, and it was no bad sign of his intelligence that the man upon whom he most relied was Collins' favourite, MacNamara. MacNamara reported him to Collins as 'brainy but at sea'. 'At sea' was right.

In the process of reorganisation Assistant Commissioner Redmond had got rid of one detective whose loyalty to the force made him feel he had a grievance. He approached Redmond with this grievance, and Redmond replied by stating his own position very bluntly. 'You were supposed to have been looking for Collins,' he said. 'You have been after him for months and never caught a sight of him, while a new man, just over from England, met him and talked to him after two days.'

This was truthful; it was scarcely discreet. The man with the grievance repeated the words to another, who mentioned them casually to MacNamara. MacNamara now began to cock his ears.

On the following day everything was ready for the capture of Collins. At the top of Brendan Road was a detective with a

86

bicycle. In Waterloo Road, a few hundred yards from O'Connor's house, was a large contingent of military and police. Tobin picked Jameson up in town, and they went to O'Connor's together. Jameson's ostensible business with Collins was soon done with, and they departed together and strolled to the top of Brendan Road to catch a city-bound tram. They both noticed the gentleman who mounted his bicycle and made off in the direction of Waterloo Road—to give warning of Collins' presence in the house alone as Jameson believed. When the tram reached Waterloo Road they saw him speaking to the police officer in charge of the convoy and noticed the soldiers make for their lorries with a rush. Tobin took fright. 'If they turn to the left it'll be Mick they're after,' he said to Jameson. From the top of the tram they looked back eagerly. The convoy of soldiers and police wheeled to the right!

Jameson's thought on this occasion must have been such as lie too deep for tears. One can only guess at his bewilderment and consternation when he saw his great chance thrown away. How was he to have known the fool of a detective had taken *him* for Collins and informed the Assistant Commissioner that Collins had left the house with Tobin?

Whereupon Fortune, having done her damnedest with Mr. Jameson, proceeded to kick him ignominiously from the human scene.

Collins had now MacNamara's report of Redmond's utterance and of the mistake which had saved his life, for MacNamara was one of the raiding party; he had, further, Tom Cullen's statement that 'whatever anyone said about him, Jameson was nothing but a crooked English bastard'. He was still unconvinced. If Jameson had reported his presence at Batt O'Connor's, then, equally, he had reported that he lunched there each day with Stack. That could be tested easily enough. He warned Mrs. O'Connor that neither he nor any of the others would be in for lunch. But at lunch time he rode as usual up Morehampton Road with Joe O'Reilly. Suddenly, as he came in sight of the waiting detective, he put on a terrific burst of speed, swept round the corner of Brendan Road, and just as quickly round the first corner on his left. Puzzled,

O'Reilly knocked at O'Connor's. Mrs. O'Connor appeared and told him Collins was not coming in for lunch. Still more puzzled, O'Reilly decided to explore. He found Collins waiting at the end of the side road.

'See anything?' asked Collins.

'No.'

'Cycle up now and have a look.'

O'Reilly cycled up to the corner. As he did so he saw from the end of Morehampton Road a convoy of lorries tearing at full speed towards him. He had scarcely got back to Collins when they thundered past and pulled up outside O'Connor's. The temptation was too good to resist. Collins left his bicycle, strode up the road, and watched them crowding in. He came back chuckling fiercely.

'We have the laugh on them now.'

Meantime Mrs. O'Connor, suspecting nothing of the plot, answered the fierce knocking. She found herself faced by a drawn revolver. Redmond brushed in past her and, levelling his gun, flung open the dining-room door. His disappointment was bitter when he saw a clear table covered with a strip of green baize—not a sign of lunch, much less of Collins. Unable to believe his eyes, he rushed upstairs, and when he came down his chagrin and rage were visible to all. His eye lit upon a picture of a group of Dail delegates; he wished to take it; she begged him not to, telling him he could get a small reproduction for a copper. Decently enough, he withdrew and said he would not trouble her again—as Beaslai points out, a most prophetic remark. But he waited that night outside the house with MacNamara, and one can only regret that MacNamara's death has deprived us of one of the most ironic scenes in history.

While Redmond argued with Mrs. O'Connor, Collins and O'Reilly were cycling down Herbert Park. At intervals Collins threw back his head and chuckled fiercely, a trick he had when anything appealed to his queer sense of humour. But all at once he fell serious. O'Reilly heard him growl something under his breath. A growl which boded ill for Mr. Jameson.

Assistant Commissioner Redmond had been staying in the

Standard Hotel, waiting until rooms could be readied for him inside the strong walls of Dublin Castle. Meanwhile he wore armour. MacNamara was now able to report that the rooms were ready, and Collins, who knew if once he got inside the Castle he would be very difficult to get out again, gave the signal for his death. After a bad mistake, when the life of an inoffensive citizen was nearly taken, two Intelligence officers trailed him home one evening from the Castle. They were taking no chances; they did not know he had left his armour behind that day; they aimed high. The first shot smashed his jaw, but, game to the last, he made a valiant attempt to draw his gun before the second finished him.

Jameson had tactfully withdrawn but returned about Christmas with a delightful Christmas present for his friends the rebels. He brought a portmanteau full of revolvers. Cullen, whose aversion for the Russian representative neither time nor circumstance had shaken, devised a simple but effective frame-up (from courting Mr. Jameson, the Volunteers had descended to fooling him). Tobin and Thornton greeted him; Thornton carried the heavy portmanteau, and Jameson was allowed to see him plainly carrying it down to Kapp and Peterson's basement in Bachelors' Walk. He was not allowed to see him shifting it five minutes later. Soon MacNamara came along with the news that a raid on the premises was timed for three o'clock. Tobin, Cullen and Thornton, from the farther side of the river, watched the raiders ransack Messrs. Kapp and Peterson's basement and depart with nothing. But so certain was Jameson of his information that they returned at midnight with picks and shovels and tore up the floors, looking for the concealed arsenal.

Mr. Jameson had presented Tobin with an Iron Cross which he declared was a decoration conferred on him by the Russian government (it now decorated the wall of the Intelligence Office) and a pass which he declared would enable Tobin to enter a barracks at any hour. He now asked for the pass to be given back. Collins saw the chance for another frame-up.

'Tell him it's in X's,' he snapped.

That night X, a Loyalist, had his house raided and was kept

shivering in his nightshirt on the doorstep. Jameson was growing desperate. He declared that the one man he wanted to kill was Churchill; but Tobin, to whom Churchill was merely a name, failed to show the appropriate reaction. Watching a raid with Tobin and Cullen, he pulled them anxiously by the sleeve with 'Let's shoot at them!' He tried all the arts of the *agent provocateur* without success. They were getting tired of him. One day he showed them a newspaper item dealing with the transport of troops to Russia.

'I think I should go over and stop that,' he said. 'Don't you think so?'

Tobin did not mind.

'Shall I do it? Would you like me to do it?' pressed Jameson.

'Oh, all right,' said Tobin to get rid of him. 'Do it, and send us a wire.'

He duly received a wire from Southampton.

Anyone but a thoroughgoing spy would have been glad to get out of trouble as easily as this, and thanked heaven for a group of soft-hearted young men with no great taste for bloodshed. But your true spy is a conceited fellow. At the end of February 1920 Mr. Jameson came back. He made further attempts to see Tobin, who was not to be seen. Collins had issued orders that while his men were not to appear as though they were avoiding him, they must keep as far as possible from the plausible possessor of the Iron Cross. He remained kicking his heels about Dublin and bought two more birds. He had made up his mind to leave Dublin when he ran into O'Reilly in the street. O'Reilly did his best to get away, but Jameson ran after him, shouting his name. He halted with death in his heart. He knew what Collins would say to this. Jameson's first words were to inquire where and when he could see Collins. O'Reilly tried to put him off.

'But I want to see him. I must see him. Can you take a letter to him?'

'He's not in town. It will take a couple of hours to reach him.'

'Never mind. I must try and see him. I'm leaving on the

boat tonight.'

O'Reilly took the note. His premonition regarding his reception was fully justified. Collins stormed. Hadn't he given instructions that Jameson was to be avoided? Was O'Reilly completely incapable of looking after himself? What sort of people had he to deal with, and what use were they to him, etc., etc.? O'Reilly bore it manfully and promised to keep out of Mr. Jameson's way for the future. He had hardly left the house when Mr. Jameson rushed across the road and stopped him. He was carrying a bird cage with a new canary; he had now three to bring back with him. What was the reply to his letter? he asked. O'Reilly, feeling as though all luck had deserted him, said the reply had not yet come. No doubt it would be along during the afternoon. In a sort of daze he made an appointment to meet Mr. Jameson at a drapers' shop in O'Connell Street at five that evening, in order to allow time for Jameson to see Collins before the boat went.

The storm he had faced before was nothing to what took place when he returned with this piece of news. Collins raged, striding up and down the room. Then he fell silent, though he still continued to stride.

'When did you say you'd meet him, and where?' he snapped.

'At five, at——,' O'Reilly faltered.

'All right. I'll show him,' said Collins and strode to the writing table. He scribbled a few lines, enclosed it in an envelope, and passed it to O'Reilly. His face was very grim as he did so.

At five O'Reilly found Mr. Jameson waiting for him at the counter of ——, a well-known Republican meeting place. He told Mr. Jameson that Collins would see him. Mr. Jameson did not conceal his glee. They were waiting, O'Reilly said, for the escort which would bring him to Collins' present headquarters. The escort was a little late. Finally they arrived, four young men, grave and silent, and O'Reilly charged them faithfully to see that Mr. Jameson was brought straight to Mick. They promised, and O'Reilly accompanied them to the tram. From the footboard Mr. Jameson, who was nothing if not polite, thanked him for his trouble, and in the cold March evening O'Rielly saw him being whirled away up O'Connell Street on a nineteen car towards Glasnevin, pleased that at last he had effected a fresh contact with Collins.

In the laneway where the escort halted he realised that he was trapped. Until a minute or two before the end he continued to bluff boldly. 'Oh, you fellows will get hell if anything happens to me,' he warned the Squad. 'Collins will deal with you! And Tobin happens to be a particular friend of mine.' Then he drew himself up to die with dignity. They asked him if he wished to pray. 'No,' he said. 'We are only doing our duty,' they told him. 'And I have done mine,' he said. As the guns were levelled he clicked his heels and stood to attention. They searched the body, but his pockets were entirely empty except for a novel by Edgar Wallace. In his rooms they found only two cases of jewelry.

The spies, having begun at all, seemed as though they must come in battalions. And the Irish are notoriously a gullible race. Mr. Jameson had come armed with an introduction from Art O'Brien. The next spy came with one from Ferran, a Republican member of parliament. He was a soldier named Fergus Brian Mulloy, stationed in the Army Pay Office at Parkgate, and over tea at Batt O'Connor's announced that his superiors were anxious he should join the Secret Service. He was willing to do so in order to provide Collins with information about its activities. But Jameson had made Collins more cautious. He left Tobin to see what could be got out of this plausible gentleman in English uniform with an English accent who professed such a desire to help his native land.

Fergus Brian Mulloy suffered from the usual weakness of spies. Tobin saw him regularly, so did Cullen and Thornton; they had tea with him in the Café Cairo, or drinks in Kidd's Restaurant, but nothing at all could they get out of him, not even a revolver or an army pass. He had promised to get some arms from Parkgate, but he left an apologetic note for Batt O'Connor, beginning 'Dear Comrade', to say that this had proved impossible.

From the very beginning the friendship seemed to be hampered by mutual distrust. Since he could not provide them with the arms they required, Fergus Brian offered to introduce Cullen and Thornton into Dublin Castle after dark and let them copy out some most important secret documents, about the contents of which he was exceedingly vague. With a distrust all the more remarkable because they continued to meet him every evening, they refused this handsome offer. The number of dark corners within the high walls of Dublin Castle probably had something to do with it. Instead, they suggested that he might help them in the job of shooting Colonel Y, the head of the Military Intelligence Department, who had quarters outside barracks. Mysteriously Colonel Y disappeared from those quarters.

Then Mulloy began to come to his interviews with Tobin accompanied by an escort, and Tobin, who had every reason to be jumpy himself, provided another escort. Distrust is no word for the relations of Tobin and Fergus Brian.

Fergus Brian, with the incredible simplicity of the spy, pressed for genuine information with which to impress his employers. He did not ask for much. Merely the location of some dump containing arms the Volunteers did not set much store by, or the hiding place of some moderate leader whose temporary absence in prison they would not be likely to miss. It was a trifling favour to ask of a real friend, but Tobin continued to be strangely disobliging.

Let it be remarked that this strange comedy was being played in the restaurants of a well-lighted street, the most fashionable in Dublin, and not more than a few hundred yards from the gates of Dublin Castle, and that, all around, Auxiliaries, Black and Tans, and British officers were drinking and dining; a few well disposed, passing on information to Collins' Intelligence officers, the rest ready to tear them limb from limb if only they knew who they were.

One evening in the Café Cairo Fergus Brian called all his powers of persuasion to his aid. He produced a pencil and a sheet of paper. Tobin looked at the paper in consternation. It was a sheet of official Dail Eireann note paper, a large quantity of which had been seized by police on a raid and was now being used, among other places, in the headquarters of the British Secret Service in Dublin Castle. It was the same note paper that was later used in the death notices issued by the Secret Service to members of Dail Eireann. Three days before, the first of the murders had taken place, that of Tom MacCurtain.

'Come now,' pressed the ingenuous Fergus Brian, 'write the address of Count Plunkett or Countess Markievicz. It won't make any difference if they are arrested, and I'll be trusted with more secrets.'

Tobin felt he was being drawn into a trap. He would write the address, the person he named would be murdered, the murderers would leave behind, as though by accident, a sheet of Dail Eireann note paper with the name and address of the victim in the handwriting of Collins' lieutenant, and Lloyd George would be able to state—as he did afterwards state about MacCurtain—that the murder had been carried out by Irish extremists.

Tobin hurriedly refused and broke off the interview, wondering if he would get away with his life from the over simple Fergus Brian.

Collins decided that Fergus Brian must go. Cullen protested. Cullen was soft hearted, and never before had they shot a man except on the most damning evidence. Look at the chances Jameson had got! But the shadow of the terror had already fallen on Collins. MacCurtain had got no mercy. He was tired of giving it.

Next evening—it was the twenty-fifth of March—Fergus Brian came to a rendezvous at the usual place in Grafton Street. No one appeared. Fergus Brian strode up and down, waiting. When he reached the top of Grafton Street he grew suddenly frightened. He was so far from the Castle! He turned on his heel and strode rapidly back. As he did so a group of men followed him. Fergus Brian quickened his stride until he was almost running. He turned up Wicklow Street; he was nearly safe now. But this was the chance the Squad had been waiting for. They rushed after him up the narrow dark street and riddled him with bullets. How far the realistic spirit of the Volunteers outpaced that of the people was shown by a massed attack upon the Squad, who had to beat their way out with drawn guns.

A few weeks later there was found in the Castle mail a letter from a relative of Fergus Brian's in California, acknowledging Captain Q——'s account of his death, and inquiring whether 'the man Tobin had yet been arrested'. Collins was interested by this. Boland was at home on a flying visit, and Collins instructed him to make inquiries about this lady when he returned to America. A curious story emerged. When Fergus Brian took up Secret-Service work he also took the precaution of making a will. In the will, which had been forwarded to his relative in America, he stated that if he met his death by violence 'a man named Tobin' would be responsible.

While regretting his lack of faith in human nature, one must acquit Fergus Brian of undue optimism.

CHAPTER IX

ENTER THE BLACK AND TANS

THE shooting of spies occupied much less of Collins' time than the previous chapter might suggest. He had more important business on hand. At the end of the year he was in London with Barton, Duffy and O'Kelly, vainly endeavouring to see President Wilson to present him with Ireland's case for freedom, but Wilson was a shy man and refused to be seen. Collins considered the idea of kidnapping him to make him listen but gave up in disgust. Plainly, Wilson would do nothing.

He had high hopes of shooting French, the English viceroy. With the development of his Intelligence Department and the detectives, he could now tell beforehand quite a lot regarding 'Johnnie's' movements and had men lying in wait for him. On one occasion he gathered a few friends at short notice and went himself to ambush the viceroy in Trinity Street, but on each occasion French took an alternative route. On the twelfth of December Collins' ambushing party caught him at Ashtown Cross. There were three cars with rifles and machine guns, but by a piece of sheer ill luck he escaped.

Boland arrived home on the twenty-seventh of May 1920 on a flying visit to explain the position of de Valera in America. There was, of course, a boisterous reunion. Collins had a new joke ready. De Valera was the G.S. (great statesman); Boland, the G.S.S. (great social success).

But, to a man facing the terror at home, the news he brought was not altogether reassuring. At first everything had gone swimmingly with the Great Statesman, who had come to rescue the Irish in America from faction; literally, it was roses all the way. But the Irish in America had a leader of their own, and de Valera did not altogether approve of him. Judge Cohalan was a ward politician of the old school. He wanted Irish freedom, but he also wanted to beat Woodrow Wilson and was using the Irish vote as a stick to beat him with. Cohalan had been suspect of pro-Germanism during the war, so he did not wish to cut a dash as an out-and-out Republican. All he would ask for Ireland was what he called Self-Determination. In opposition to him stood MacCartan, an old 1916 man, and his friends. They wanted America to recognise the Irish Republic.

De Valera was not quite sure what he wanted. Conscious at first, possibly under the moderating influence of Griffith, of a certain danger in the Declaration of Independence, he was out for Self-Determination. Then, as reception followed reception, and the title of President of the Irish Republic attached itself to him, willy-nilly, he began to toy with recognition. Recognition was the last thing the Cohalanites wanted. They were loyal American citizens, and President de Valera got on their nerves. At last de Valera gave an interview in which he was imprudent enough to mention Cuban autonomy as a form of association with England on which he might agree. Cohalan and Devoy, galled by his previous behaviour and his growing prestige, saw the chance of discrediting him. Devoy denounced him for letting down the Irish cause. De Valera, hastily abandoning his new found moderation, did exactly what he did later in the Treaty debates when Document Number 2 met with disfavour—he beat a hurried retreat to extreme Republicanism; he has always been tactician enough to know that no one will fight for a compromise. Cohalan and Devoy, also abandoning their rather perilous Republicanism, became more emphatic than ever in favour of Self-Determination.

As occurred in the later split, a minute dash of principle provided the excuse for a flood of viciousness and folly. It was, in fact, a foreshadowing of the Treaty split; the first rift in the magnificent pretence of the Republic, the first intimation that behind its apparent solidarity was not a nation but a nation in the making, the majority of whose citizens were demanding the Republic in the tone in which a farmer at the fair declares before God that nothing less than fifteen pounds will he take for a beast which all know he will be glad to sell for ten.

It was only another tragic result of the Declaration of Independence. A previous one had resulted in a cleavage between Brugha and Collins. Brugha had demanded that the Oath of Allegiance be administered to the Volunteers, who were now the standing army of the Republican government. On the face of it nothing could be more reasonable, and, as well as physical-force men like Terry MacSwiney of Cork, Brugha had Griffith on his side; because Griffith hoped that by making the Volunteers subject to the Dail cabinet the extremists could be forced to toe the line. But Collins knew perfectly well that Brugha wanted to tie up not only the Volunteers but the secret society which Collins controlled. He had never liked it. Now he hoped to smash it by making its members, who were mostly Volunteers, swear allegiance to the Dail.

Now the constitution of the Republican Brotherhood pledged its allegiance not to the Dail but to its own Supreme Council, which was held to be the *de jure* government of Ireland. Collins was the Supreme Council, and in exchange for that absolute authority he was being asked to content himself with such authority as his position on de Valera's rickety

97

cabinet afforded him. But he could not fight both Brugha and Griffith; the oath had been made mandatory at the Dail meeting in August of the previous year, and though Collins still, to Brugha's indignation, continued to utilise the Republican Brotherhood, the harm was done. Not only had the two leaders, idealist and realist, come to open conflict, but hundreds of Collins' men were compelled to take an oath which, like Brugha, they interpreted in a nakedly literal way.

Boland's report, which strongly favoured de Valera, was accepted by Collins and the Republican Brotherhood, because Boland was their representative, and no suspicion entered their minds that Boland, who had left Ireland devoted to Collins, had now transferred his allegiance. Griffith, too, accepted it, because de Valera was being attacked by Devoy and Cohalan for his moderation, and Griffith was a moderate. Brugha, Markievicz and Plunkett—it should be remembered to their credit—would willingly have repudiated de Valera's Cuban autonomy speech, but Collins and Griffith succeeded in getting them to accept his explanation—this also to their credit—for the tragic issue unknown to all was already knit, and the only question was on which side the Chief Executive would fall.

Their discussions went on in an atmosphere of thickening menace. The men and women who sat there knew it was no longer a question of arrest and imprisonment. Since the great famine of 1848 Ireland experienced no such accumulation of horrors as descended on her in 1920. Collins, with his gift for incisive phrasing, summed it up as 'which would last longer, the body or the lash', and, reverting to his favourite idea, he said, 'As always, the battleground is here at home, and, to my mind, it is now a question of our own nerves.'

The men at home needed all the nerve they could muster. Up to this Collins had to deal only with the Detective Division of the Metropolitan Police. Fergus Brian, that melancholy soul, ushered in a new dispensation, and Collins—a country lad of twenty-nine, a Post Office clerk—found himself matched against the whole of the English Secret Service, whose agents covered the globe, and whose funds and resources were inexhaustible.

It is a chastening thought for utopians that every form of government—rabid dictatorship, merchant republic, workers' republic, even democratic state—exists at all, thanks only to this power—which we never see, which wears no uniform, clanks no sword, has no public register and no competitive examination. Parliaments may say who shall govern openly; they may not say who shall govern in secret; they may not even know. Most often we become aware of it only in history, and then we are shocked, but the veils are lifted so gradually that it seems as though such horrible things existed only long ago or far away. The priest who betrayed his flock for money, the genial writer of plays who, having sold his dearest friend, came to console him in the condemned cell—these things are part of the history of the eighteenth century and what we are pleased to call a venal age, but in a hundred years time (unless rulers adopt the Irish habit of burning files) what secrets may not come to light concerning our most innocent-seeming neighbours?

Intelligence officers began to invade Ireland, some secretly, some with what was intended to be secrecy. A party of priests returning from Rome was joined by a strange man who began to say his rosary. He told them he was going to Ireland because of its splendid Catholicism. He was allowed to see very little else. In squalid public houses English voices solemnly prefaced each remark with 'Bedad', 'Begorra', or 'Bejabers' —to reassure the natives. Money began to flow like water, and poor half-illiterate men, ex-soldiers, corner boys and tramps acted as touts. They wandered through the country on specious errands. In the early morning passing carmen found them lying under a ditch with a bandage about their eyes. On those obscure tragedies the veil is seldom lifted, but here and there in official reports we catch a glimpse of them and hear the faltering voice of the victim as he faces some burly country boy with a revolver.

'Seeing that I had him found out in his manoeuvres, he asked for forgiveness, saying that he would have no more to do with the government if I let him go. I told him it was too many chances he got, and he asked for one more chance. I then

99

told him to prepare for confession, and I went to a Priest and brought him forward after he had his confession told. The priest called me one side and asked me did I hold court-martial on him, and I told him I did; he said that was right, that I was doing my duty. The priest then gave him the Blessed Sacrament, and he told me to take him out immediately out of his sight.'

Poor creatures, often they did not even know the value of the blood money they earned. This is another tout, confessing before he, too, faced the revolver.

'I gave information to an English officer in —— of the raid on —— about six months ago. I said my brother was in motor with other men and these were the men who raided the barracks. The officer asked me what these men were doing, and I said taking arms. I said that those men's names were —— (my brother), ——, and ——. The officer gave me fifty pounds and told me to continue getting things. I put this money in the bank after keeping one pound. I can't count but I put in the remainder of the money.'

These men and their employers were the people Collins had to watch throughout the length and breadth of Ireland, and within a month or two the struggle between two opposing parties, which looked at one time as though it might develop into open warfare, changed into a savage battle between two Secret Services, fought out without mercy in the darkness.

Dublin was put under a curfew regulation, partly to restrict the operations of the Volunteers, but principally to allow the English Secret Service men greater freedom of movement. This, of course, cut both ways. Collins instructed his friends among the uniformed police to mark every man who walked the streets at night.

In broad daylight he had their mail seized. During the spring the murder clubs organised. On the twentieth of March 1920 police entered the house of MacCurtain, the Lord Mayor of Cork, and killed him before the eyes of his wife. Lloyd George declared the work to be that of Sinn Fein extremists. It was unfortunate that he could not have had MacCurtain's address in the handwriting of Collins' lieutenant by way of evidence.

Collins was after the murderers hotfoot. From Wexford he traced a car of English Intelligence officers to the roadway outside MacCurtain's house, and thence to Thurles, where within a few days other murders took place. He thought he knew the identity of one of these officers. He had already captured a letter from an Intelligence officer in Ireland addressed to him in Whitehall and containing a reference to 'our little stunt'.* Another of the murderers he identified as the local inspector, Swanzy, who was shortly afterwards shifted to a safe billet in the north of Ireland. Collins had him followed and killed.

While the MacCurtain murder was being planned elsewhere, the Castle was filled with anxiety to lay hands on the considerable sums which, in spite of proscription and confiscation, Collins had collected and banked under the names of private individuals. An inspector named Bell was brought from Belfast to trace these funds. On the first of March he issued a proclamation calling upon bank managers to appear before him and give evidence regarding the source of their deposits. It was now only a question of time until he laid hands upon the National Loan. Collins had collected that money; and it was not in the least likely that he would allow even the most excellent father of a family to get away with it. With less compunction than he had ever shown, he sent the Intelligence officers to get Mr. Bell. Mr. Bell proved difficult to get. He was protected by his innocuous appearance which made him difficult to identify. The Intelligence officers even doubted Collins story that Mr. Bell was seen to his tram each morning at Monkstown and escorted from it at Nassau Street by detectives—that seemed too gross a piece of stupidity even for Dublin Castle. But one morning, as they waited at the top of Sandymount Avenue, a cyclist rode up to say that a man answering Mr. Bell's description was coming into town on the next tram. The Intelligence officers boarded it, four of them, and sat near an inoffensive little businessman, the only one who seemed to fit the description. What did they think of that

* Beaslai: op. cit.

horse for the 2.30? one asked cryptically. Someone said doubt-fully that he was the favourite, but another snapped 'a dead cert' and had him by the throat. They struggled at the door, and all pitched on to the road together. Mr. Bell would prove a terror to no further bank managers.

When O'Reilly came in that evening Collins had just heard the news from Cullen and, strained beyond endurance by the long quest for Mr. Bell, was beside himself with rage. O'Reilly, devotion and all, was at the end of his tether; sleep-less nights and heartbreaking labour from dawn to dark were proving too much for him. He wept like a child. He told Collins that he was going and not coming back.

'All right,' growled Collins. 'Take some dispatches for me on your way.'

The girl to whom O'Reilly brought the dispatches asked the reason for his tear-stained face and he broke down again. She went at once to Collins and denounced him for not even realising how O'Reilly worked. Collins was outraged and indignant. 'You mind your own damn business!' he shouted. 'I know how O'Reilly works.' And, of course, O'Reilly was back at work next morning.

In quick succession he got rid of two more detectives and the officer who had ill-treated Clarke in 1916, now a police officer in Gorey. People were growing accustomed to the new departure, and Holy Ireland with its flamboyant romanticism and queasy conscience was rapidly going under. And it struck terror into the remaining policemen. When the Secret Service men took over, there were few of the old persuasion who could or would help them. Collins had scored the first point by forcing them to begin from scratch. In May 1920 they issued death notices to all the Irish members of parliament. They were typed on the paper seized from Dail Eireann head-quarters.

Then came the Black and Tans. The pressure on the old police, the ambushes, captures of barracks, propaganda and social ostracism had forced large numbers to resign. It was mostly the older men, near pension time, who stayed on, and if they wished for their pensions they hoped also that they might live to enjoy them, so they were dumb. Only strong garrisons could now hold the barracks—which had been turned into fortresses with sandbags, steel shutters and barbed wire—and as these were evacuated or captured the buildings were fired. English rule was being gradually forced back upon the cities and big towns, and even in these there was a desperate shortage of men and a continuous feeling of insecurity; fighting had turned the Volunteers from a mob into something like a trained army; they were acquiring skill and initiative, and it was not beyond possibility that the home-made mines and bombs which had made smithereens of substantial buildings might be used in time against the towns themselves.

To remedy this Lloyd George drew upon the bravos, the bullies, ex-convicts and ne'er-do-wells to maintain the peace in Ireland. They were a force calculated to inspire terror in a population less timid and law abiding than the Irish. With their indeterminate uniforms—black tunics and khaki trousers or khaki tunics and black trousers—and revolvers carried in cowboy holsters, they looked like something which had walked off the stage during a performance of *The Beggar's Opera*. Here a man had a patch over one eye, there walked another who had a hook for a hand, and one face in six proclaimed that its owner was cheating the public hangman. There was no question of discipline; that was not required. They robbed and blackguarded wholesale.

But the pick of the bunch were the Auxiliaries or Cadets. These were supposed to be ex-officers; they wore Glengarry caps and were paid double the salary of the ordinary Black and Tan for an accent savouring more of the public school and a greater savagery and recklessness. They were the picked forces of empire, and, like the Volunteers, they elected their own officers. In a curious way the Irish, who like a good fighter, respected them. Time and time again the Volunteers testified to their bravery, but too often the mangled corpse of a woman or an old man did as much for their savagery.

These were the agents employed for the reconquest of Ireland, and their arrival let hell loose on a distracted people. A year before, the popular representatives were wanted to serve a three months sentence. Now they were shot or tortured. Collins might well say it was the body or the lash. He grinned and made new demands upon his mighty will power. His nerves had to be controlled. He gave up smoking. He had to keep his wits about him. He gave up casual drinking. He had to concentrate. He took up Pelmanism. No one but Collins would have answered such a challenge with Pelmanism. It is one of the most illuminating slants we have on his peculiar view of the Revolution.

He did not allow the new terror to impede his movements any more than the old. He even attended race meetings in the Phoenix Park with Cullen and others of the Intelligence Staff. On one occasion to his great delight he backed a rank outsider, called 'Irish Republic' which astonished everyone by coming in at fifty to one. He was up and about long before Auxiliaries or Volunteers, shooting through the deserted streets on his bicycle. He spent the morning at his Intelligence Office. The first half-hour was spent in clearing up work left over from the previous day. Then O'Reilly arrived with the day's papers, Irish and English. They included *The Times* and the *Morning Post*. He went through them carefully, noting developments of political or military interest. Meanwhile O'Reilly opened the day's dispatches, stamped them with the day's date and pinned them neatly to the envelopes. Collins went through them, paragraphing with a coloured pencil—the instinctive protest of his neat mind against the wholesale disorder which faced him. He dictated replies, his eyes upon the window but seeing nothing. It was as though he were visualising what he wished to say and reading it from the imaginary printed page. He never needed to revise. When quoting a letter he never paraphrased; no matter how long, the paragraph had to be written out in full, so that there could be no shadow of doubt as to what was in question. A code knock at the door and the typist from his Finance Office appeared with correspondence from the previous day to be signed.

After lunch he had to see his Intelligence officers, his warders, railwaymen, or seamen; he had to visit his Finance Office to deal with the day's business. As he cycled through the streets he passed searching parties of soldiers, Black and Tans and Auxiliaries. Sometimes they stopped and searched him, and then he usually had a brief chat with them and proffered an encouraging word or two, more particularly if they happened to be looking for himself. 'Attaboy! Go and get him!' he said as he mounted his bicycle again. When Fitzgerald called him from his bicycle to warn him that the road was held by Auxiliaries, Collins said, 'There are several of those fellows I don't know yet. I'll just go and have a look.'

From tea until bedtime—which always meant curfew time —it was the same, unless he had decided to take the evening off and go to the theatre. There was a crowd waiting for him in Vaughan's Hotel; messengers with loan funds; Intelligence officers with reports; officers from the country seeking arms or ammunition; political men. He went through them one by one, sometimes taking a brief note. His decisions were rapped out like lightning and never altered. His memory for detail was phenomenal. He remembered even the duty hours of friendly postmen and could say where an important packet might be posted and for what collection. Fifty or a hundred letters (single associates in Dublin received as many as six in the course of a day); dozens of interviews, each letter and interview dealing perhaps with as many as a dozen different subjects, each of which was as urgent as such things can be only in the middle of a war; the whole extending perhaps to four or five countries and involving the lives of hundreds of men and thousands of pounds, every penny of which, as Minister for Finance, he would have to account for—not always to sympathetic colleagues, as events proved. People became used to the sudden violent dive into the breast pocket for his notebook and hurriedly penned note. Orderly in all things, he seldom used a pencil. He hated letters addressed in pencil, and raised hell's delight if he got one signed with a rubber stamp.

And the endless variety of this business. —— must interview the Bishop of —— and try to get that subscription from him; —— of Glasgow has an offer of .303 ammunition, and is the price excessive? —— [an English Communist], having brought ammunition for the Irish to Liverpool, has been trailed and lost by Scotland Yard men, so —— receives Scotland Yard's report upon his activity a day or two later. Neil Kerr, his Liverpool agent, is ill, and Collins, who never forgets anyone, must secure a bed in a Dublin nursing home for him, so that he can call on the patient each day; a gentleman called —— is keen to secure for the Irish cause the £75,000 which Lenin is supposed to have allocated to an English newspaper; —— of Manchester is having difficulties about the supply of faked passports for leaders on their way to America; a gentleman called —— reports that four Volunteers in his home town had taken him from his bed and robbed him of £24; that was because his wife was unfaithful to him. Through it there runs as strange a gallery of characters as the mind of the wildest sensationalist could desire, and each of these has to be checked up on; spies, adventurers on the make, fanatics and plain lunatics.

Here is the inevitable Secret Service man turning up at an Irish centre in England. 'Smith was not his correct name (it so rarely is!) but he stated from his experiences in Ireland, especially what he found out regarding the plans of the government, he wanted to pass on his information. He said he can furnish names and addresses of the principal Secret Service agents (both English and Irish), also their secret signs of recognition and their, as he termed it, "phraseology".'

It is all disposed of in a luminous, businesslike, yet quite personal style which is in striking contrast to his longer utterances. His ordinary prose style is far from good; though often interesting and always forceful, it is cumbrous, emotional and blurred. In it we see the Collins of the public platform, a man all temperament. In his dispatches there is rarely a blurring, rarely a straying outside the edges; though immensely detailed, they are always beautifully clear. It is part of the dichotomy which makes him so interesting; just as this big, blustering, violent nature transmutes itself in the feminine precision and delicacy of his relations with people who are poor or in trouble, so does the man whom Churchill saw as if straight from a backwoods camp turn his violent emotionalism into labour so exact and detailed that it seems to have been

106

performed under a mental microscope.

Only occasionally does the nightmare of his daily existence transpire, or a troubled sentence indicate that those model business letters were written by a man with a revolver at his elbow, who yesterday had escaped death by an inch and was now facing out into streets filled with touts and cut-throats, all hoping for the enormous reward offered for his life. When there is a sigh it is for some friend. 'I have not very much heart in what I am doing today, thinking of poor Thomas [MacCurtain]. It is surely the most appalling thing that has been done yet.' In dealing with him, his agents seem inspired to the same ruthless suppression of self. 'I arrived back in Liverpool all right on Tuesday morning to find the son of Joseph Plunkett dead a few hours before I arrived. It was not unexpected. Enclosed also is receipts for the two amounts that I received by P. on the 23rd.'

Yet the eternal boy in Collins cannot resist a whoop of exultation whenever a Cork team wins at Croke Park. 'In my opinion they are the finest combination that ever played in Croke Park. The Dublin team was simply not in the picture.'

No wonder if his relaxation has become legendary. Of course he was always up to antics. No joke was too crude or simple for him. In Vaughan's Hotel he took the boots of early departing travellers and replaced them from above. In a pub his favourite device was to dodge his call; in a hotel, to let some pal in for the bill; when the bill was paid he diverted attention as he coolly pocketed the change. He borrowed or invented impossible scandalous stories about his friends. His very speech was an obstacle race of obscure jokes, slang, native Irish words like *drœvuoil*, such as arise naturally in the speech of West Cork, or coined words like 'Oggs', his farewell, based on a friend's pronunciation of *Slán agaibh*. He loved nick-names and diminutives—Piersheen, Cahileen, Dickeen; Cosgrave was 'Cosgar' or simply 'James's Street'.

He delighted his friends with his incalculable fantastic wit. Once in a public house he saw an argumentative soul whose elbow, as he grew more impassioned, edged closer to his glass. Collins watched it in fascination. Then he gently pushed the argumentative soul away.

'Excuse me,' he said, 'I'd rather see a church fall.'

Cullen, who was a champion runner, came in for a lot of it. A Press photographer once succeeded in photographing him with his head over his shoulder. Collins, a runner himself, knew what that meant. Next day Collins, finding him in a pub, professed to be shocked.

'Honest to God, Mick, I'm sober,' he declared. 'Look, I can walk straight!'

'You can't run straight though,' said Collins with a grin.

And, of course, he was a confirmed and irresponsible tease. His great delight was to cause the most extreme embarrassment. When an officer appointed to a position on Headquarters Staff lost the entire files within five minutes of taking over, Collins, once he had laid hands on them, could not forbear demanding their return on the pretence that he had some alterations to make, merely for the pleasure of watching him squirm. He ordered his secretary to increase her salary by ten shillings a week and then gravely queried the salary returns on the ground that he had not appointed a date for the increase. He insisted on being supplied with dinner when he knew the larder was empty. When he came to the theatre he usually appeared first in the cashier's desk, pretending to grab the cash. Those schoolboyish jokes and bubbling high spirits made him an uncomfortable companion.

But it was really only when the day's work was over and he was alone with the gang that his temperament got full play. Then he pushed the sofa at O'Sullivan. O'Sullivan pushed it back. O'Connor lent a hand. Tobin joined in, and the senior officers of the Irish Republican Army rolled about the floor. Collins became again the young savage of Stafford Gaol. All-in wrestling did not bear comparison, and a rugby scrum was only child's play to it. 'A bit of ear' was the goal.

The others were a rough lot, but Collins always hurt, said one of their number long after. There was only one way to tackle Collins. You had to lose your temper and hurt him first.

Nothing was sacred. In 'exercise', as he called it, Collins

108

would hurl the water croft, the wash-basin, the furniture—
anything that came to his hand. And woe betide the more
sensitive of the gang! Collins would probably willingly have
laid down his life for any of them, but even the beloved
O'Hegarty, the subtlest of all his friends, with whom he
discussed every plan that required brains, would be dragged
about the floor by the hair. His companions locked the door
against him as the only way of escaping him. They piled
furniture against it. It was all no use. When he had tried in
vain to burst in the door with his powerful shoulders—a
broken lock meant as little to him as a broken vessel—he
mounted a chair, pushed up the fanlight and with a powerful
fire extinguisher drenched the unfortunate O'Hegarty to the
skin. And all the while through pitch dark streets prowled
soldiers and Auxiliaries on rubber-soled boots, and every now
and again there came a challenge and a burst of rifle fire or the
roar of an approaching Lancia car.

Yet his hosts adored him. There was Devlin and his wife,
between whom and Collins there sprang up one of those
intense relationships which only he seemed capable of inspir-
ing. When Devlin met Collins he handed over a neatly furnished room. Within a month it was a wreck. There was
scarcely a chair with a back to it; the delph had disappeared.
Yet when one of the gang, hearing a tumble and thunder from
the sitting room in which Collins was lashing out with a chair,
apologised to the Devlins, they merely smiled and said, 'it eases
his mind.'

They spoke with the understanding of love, for it was in this
savage lashing and straining that all the accumulated anxiety
was released. In the tumult of it, still echoing after fifteen
years, there is something which resembles the elephantine
capering of a Beethoven scherzo. And in the lightnings which
flash from the heart of a scherzo there is something that resembles Collins' daemonic rages.

Even in boyhood, as I have shown, the thing people noticed
was his bad temper. But in the midst of his work as a soldier-
politician, away from all his London associates with the exception of Joe O'Reilly, the bad temper became externalised;

people forgot the source from which it sprang unless they happened to tread very violently indeed upon Collins' corns; and the greater the strain, the worse grew the temper, so that it became isolated, extreme, a phenomenon. He could be good humoured, restrained and dignified, but even then to discerning ears the rumblings of the interior volcano were rarely absent, and when he had to deal only with intimate friends, with whom he felt no necessity to be on his guard, the lava was always very close to the surface, and the rumblings and growlings ripped the air with only an occasional break.

It is not always easy to measure the exact significance of his rages. To some extent they were justified by the circumstances; for a considerable part they were bound up with a certain histrionic flamboyant streak in his nature. Sensitive people disliked his cruel baiting of O'Reilly and Tom Cullen. O'Malley writes: 'He had a habit of baiting Tom Cullen, the assistant quartermaster, and a few of the Dublin men that I hated. I could understand, take or make use of a tell-off, but the prodding got on my nerves. One day I told Collins I would not stand it and left the room in a rage. He never baited anyone in my presence afterwards.' Certainly those storms imposed a sort of rough-and-ready discipline on a force which was only too ready to kick over the traces. When Cullen, waltzing about the room with a typist, heard the Big Fellow's characteristic bound upon the stair he hurled the typist back to her machine and buried his face in a paper. Unpunctuality was the capital sin. Collins would be at the door like a fury, his jaw stuck out, his watch swinging wildly in his hand, to ask what the so-and-so you meant by keeping him waiting. The time element nearly always played a large part in his plans; with all the odds against success, the only hope was in an organisation perfected down to the smallest detail. For one moment of the day five men could achieve what for the rest of the time five hundred could not achieve. 'In a job like ours you must think of everything,' he said, and in one of his letters he writes, 'What a little detail causes a disaster often—in fact, it is usually the details that do it.'

His temper was so volatile that he would burst into tears at

110

one moment and roar with laughter the next, tear a man to tatters and then embrace him. One of his friends, after some slight failure for which he was not responsible, was received with a tempestuous scowl which within the space of one sentence changed to the sunniest of smiles.

'Confound you, anyway, but you did your best.'

But it was only the duds who bore malice. Nervous men, strolling through O'Connell Street, resented that hearty whack on the shoulder and the conspiratorial whisper in which Collins invited them to join him immediately in blowing up a barracks—there was a danger that he might mean it—and it was only later they realised the impish glee with which he had made them squirm and say they had a pressing appointment.

He had the capacity for arousing not only devotion but jealousy. One was conscious of the little feuds among his intimates; there was, for instance, constant friction between the men of brains and the men of action. It even transferred itself to the seamen. And when these were compelled to report to the Q.M.G. instead of to Collins, they began to grumble.

'Whatever you do,' he wrote feelingly to one of his agents, 'don't be nursing grievances. No good ever came of that.'

Yet, for all his apparent bullying, no one could attract or hold devotion as he could. Perhaps because of the bullying. He took the simplest men, men whom no one in the world had ever attached importance to, and made them feel that the smallest task they performed was a matter of life and death. Before him, after him, none could give them the same sense of responsibility, and their devotion to him was no greater than his to them. Passionate, vibrating, that tenderness of his runs through the whole story of his brief life, and each time one rediscovers it with a queer thrill. One such story occurs to me.

Dick Barrett was going upon a dangerous task. He looked longingly at a turquoise-coloured fountain pen in Collins' pocket. 'I'd like that pen,' he confessed. 'Well, you won't get it,' snapped Collins. Everyone in the room was conscious that it was not the pen Barrett wanted; it was a souvenir. 'I'll wrestle you for it,' said Collins with a grin. For a while they wrestled on the floor. Collins was powerful enough to have thrown Barrett across the room. Instead, he let himself be pinned down, and Barrett went off triumphantly with the pen.

CHAPTER X

REALISTS AND DREAMERS

STACK had made himself a nuisance to Collins. Even after his release they had been for a time the best of friends, but friends noticed a change in the courteous and gentle Stack; he had grown morose and sensitive. In prison he had become recognised as an admirable leader of obstreperousness. Whenever the prisoners made demands that they knew the prison governor could not grant they sent Stack to see him. But as Minister for Home Affairs he was a failure. The Volunteers had given him a police force, but he did nothing with it, and whenever an outbreak of crime occurred they were compelled to deal with it from their own local headquarters and employ men who already had enough to do in fighting the English. It is true that his department, like every other department of Dail Eireann, was hampered by the atmosphere of make-believe. The man had to make believe he was a minister, that his police were real police, his courts real courts, and his punishments real punishments. It is true that any power it had came from the almost hysterical tension of the people, their stubborn will to accept any law but English law. But Collins suffered as much from it as Stack, and it was just because so much make believe was necessary that a realist was required; a man who would take the whole crazy scheme in deadly earnest and work it for all it was worth. This Stack would not do. He affected to think that if by some oversight the appointment of a local chief of police was not notified to him he had no further responsibility for the district. Pakenham shows Collins solicitously inquiring of Stack if he had staff enough and,

112

when Stack amiably agreed that he had, throwing down a bundle of complaints. Everyone agreed upon the mordant comment that followed. 'Austin, your department is only a —— joke!'*

But it would be a mistake to imagine that it was only Collins who kicked. The whole personnel of general headquarters, men whom circumstances forced to be realists, had a grudge against Stack. His name occurs again and again in their files. Here is an indictment in one such report:

'The Home Affairs and Judicial departments yielded to the first onset of the enemy.... The plain fact is that our civil service have simply played at governing a republic.'

The adjutant general summed up the protest of the staff in one letter which deserves to be historic. It begins with the solemn warning:

To be returned if not understood.
The Adjutant General tells
The Chief of Staff to tell
The Minister for Defence to tell
The Minister for Home Affairs

that the Adjutant General got the letter written by the Minister for Home Affairs on the 31st ult., that in his letter the Minister for Home Affairs expressed his fear that the Home Affairs court then sitting in Cork might be captured, that the

Minister for Home Affairs wished the
Adjutant General to tell
The Adjutant, Cork No. 1 Brigade, to tell
Secretary of Sinn Fein to tell
City Registrar

that the office of Home Affairs in Dublin had been captured. . . .

* Pakenham: *Peace by Ordeal.*

113

Brugha, a much more vital figure, was equally useless. As Minister for Defence he should have attended headquarters meetings regularly but didn't; and when he interviewed a group of country officers it was usually to address them upon the importance of studying Irish. Even with regard to Irish, which he was passionately interested in, Collins did not think him practical enough. On one occasion the cabinet had under discussion a scheme which Brugha supported, and Collins, with his desire to have a hand in everything, criticised more than the other thought necessary. Brugha, with unfailing politeness—the boxer's watchful good humour—listened.

'Perhaps you'll produce a scheme for Irish yourself, Mr. Collins?'

'I will,' said Collins angrily.

'That's excellent!'

'And maybe 'twill surprise you,' growled Collins.

In a moment he had forgotten the tiff. But Brugha hadn't. At the next meeting of the cabinet he said pleasantly:

'I believe Mr. Collins' scheme for Irish will surprise us.'

'Oh, shut up!' grumbled Collins, alarmed that anyone could retain spite against him, who retained it against none.

'Oh, but, Mr. Collins, I was only quoting your own words.'

But it was on poor Stack that Collins visited most of his wrath. Few of the Cabinet liked his behaviour to Stack, as courteous and decent a man as ever breathed. And Stack resented it, fiercely but silently. In August of 1920 Collins distinguished himself over Stack's Rent Restriction Bill. Admittedly it was an unwise measure, but Stack was Collins' friend and fellow Minister, and he was far from being the only offender.

When the meeting was over, Stack and Collins met.

'That's a nice way you treated me,' said Stack half smiling.

'Well,' growled Collins, already beginning to repeat, 'you deserved it.'

'All right,' said Stack with the same half-smile, 'I'll get even with you.'

There was now occasional friction in the cabinet—between Collins on the one hand and Brugha and Stack on the other.

Apart from the personal factors which tended to deepen it, there was the clash already alluded to between the realists and opportunists like Collins and the idealists like Brugha. It was an extraordinarily clean-cut break, even though there was little overt friction. The idealists were the last of the romantics. The greatest of them was then dying on hunger strike in Brixton Prison, and his terrible protest was exciting the whole world. At one point in the struggle MacSwiney had come to headquarters and asked permission for a local rising, another '16 in Cork. His idea was that when it was stifled, as it would soon be, in blood, another should take place in Galway, and so on! MacSwiney was bidden to capture three police barracks instead. He captured them. But in all MacSwiney's actions, as indeed in all Brugha's, there was a fervid nobility; in all Collins', a hard sense and warm humanity. It is hardly likely that Collins cottoned on to MacSwiney (how could he have liked anyone whose letters had first to be translated into English for him?) his view of life, as expressed in *Principles of Freedom*, he would certainly have regarded as priggish. Neither did MacSwiney cotton on to him. His friendship he reserved for Mulcahy, whom he thought 'the only great man among the leaders'.

Each drew different types to himself, and within the revolutionary organisation there were already two worlds, two philosophies, running in very doubtful harness. While MacSwiney was dying it was decided to kill an English minister by way of reprisal. It was probably Brugha's idea. From the very start, as witness his fathering of the same notion during the conscription crisis, his panacea was a campaign against the British cabinet. A young Volunteer officer in the country threw up his position and volunteered for the job. He received £100 to support himself and his men in London while they took their bearings. Finally it was decided to kill a certain minister at a function in Oxford. The men were intercepted in Oxford itself by messengers sent out by Collins to stop them. The young officer returned to Dublin. He went to Brugha and paid over what remained of the £100. Brugha checked each item of expenditure, issued a receipt, and finally gave him his fare home.

While he was seated in the train he saw one of Collins' men peering in every carriage. It was a messenger with a cheque for £30—recompense for his wasted time and lost employment. The young man returned it. He preferred Brugha's way. It is the old story of the five-pound note for Joe Kavanagh. And yet, what is one to say? Is it not as easy to picture that young man going home, penniless and embittered by Brugha's apparent lack of appreciation?

Collins always had a notable understanding of the minor ridiculous necessities of men and women, the headaches and heartaches which money or attention could mend. When he heard from Tobin that two of his men were sleeping on bare boards in a deserted room he had mattresses sent in to them. Whenever there were difficulties about money and others were shocked or annoyed, Collins sympathised and understood.

Of course the position was embittered by Devoy, who, to further his hatred of de Valera, had cracked Collins up as 'Commander-in-Chief'. Brugha, as Minister for Defence, resented this; later, Republican propaganda proclaimed him as 'the man who beat the Black and Tans'; but even had he wished it, and been able for the job, he could not now seriously have diminished Collins' power. Collins ran Finance; the I.R.B. (the secret organisation which in spite of his efforts Brugha could not bring under the control of the Dail); the famous Squad or A.S.U.—'my Black and Tans' as Collins called them; Intelligence, which was practically shouldering the whole war; while through his agents in the ports and on the ships he practically controlled all activities abroad. Until well on in the following year almost every gun, every pound of ammunition, every ton of coke for the bomb factories, had passed through Collins' hands. Yet this does not by any means exhaust the total of his activities. He looked after the defence of court martial prisoners and the needs of their relatives; kept in touch with them through the warders; organised and maintained his own lines of communication—and remained so human that while Mrs. O'Connor's husband was lying dangerously near to death, he came each night for a week and sat with her and played with the children: went so far even as to shake her by the hand when he left, a formality he detested and dispensed with as often as possible. Week after week, at terrible risk, he went to Mrs. de Valera's at Greystones, paid her her allowance with his own hands, played with the children, and reported to his absent chief.

General Headquarters consisted mostly of his own friends, and the various directors saw without surprise Collins' frequent invasions of their preserves. They found that orders had been issued from their departments without their knowledge and accepted the position philosophically. They saw their files neatly marked 'D.B.I.', Collins' new slogan, which meant 'Don't Butt In'. But they also knew that any invasions on their part would result in a storm; it was the old story of Collins, the tease who mustn't be teased, growing up. He had a mania for secrecy. Even his closest associates were never aware of more than a fraction of his contacts; unless many more tongues are loosened it is highly doubtful if even posterity will know. On the occasion of one of his visits to England a colleague had been asked to look after his office. When Collins returned he flew into a rage because so little had been done. Nothing could have been done because he had left instructions that on no account must his *locum tenens* have access to the secret files. Even when his superior, Mulcahy, was left in charge, he was allowed to see only routine dispatches. Sometimes colleagues like O'Hegarty and O'Sullivan accidentally stumbled upon his lines and were rudely turned off. 'Don't proceed further with this,' to Tobin or Cullen, was the only indication they had that they, too, had unwittingly unearthed one of his many contacts.

I have already described his rage when he found himself being followed by the devoted O'Reilly. The same fate awaited anyone he even suspected of curiosity. Sometimes he varied his tactics with stupid people and invented Gyntian romances. But to the curiosity of old people he was always tender.

It was not only outside himself; one can feel his own mind was divided into watertight compartments. To Broy he said,

117

'Never let one side of your mind know what the other is doing.' His organisation was a working model of this. For a long time Tobin and Cullen were quite unaware of his relationship with Broy and MacNamara. On one occasion they actually shadowed them. They, in turn, went in constant danger from the ordinary Volunteer Intelligence officers. Under one name they drank with English officers and Auxiliaries in Kidd's Restaurant by day; and under another, hid from them at night; and were so often reported to Collins as enemy agents that he had to issue instructions to prevent them being shot at sight. One may say now that not only had he political detectives working for him in Dublin Castle—he had at least one prominent official, an Englishman. They had met casually in the Gresham Hotel, liked one another, and separated, ignorant of one another's identity. A few days later the Englishman received a letter which reached him within the walls of the Castle, though by none of the ordinary channels; of course, MacNamara had brought it in. Conscious of his own power, he sometimes played at mystification like this. One English Secret Service man, friendly to the Volunteers, while on holiday in England received a note from the leader of the local Irishmen informing him that his safety was being guaranteed.

It was this power of committing things to separate compartments of the mind that enabled him to forget himself so thoroughly and play the peculiar game he described to O'Connor of not allowing himself to think he was hunted. It was an essential part of his disguise. It was as though he were concealing things from himself in order to conceal them from others. Batt O'Connor describes his own agony of impatience whenever Collins threw open the door without a preliminary glance and tramped buoyantly down a silent street, clashing the iron of his heel against the flagstones. He abominated precautions—clerical clothes, false moustaches, whispers or timidity—and was always sarcastic about them. 'I'm after meeting a detective,' he declared acidly, 'and he said, "For God's sake, will you tell —— to take off his false moustache?"'

Once again Brugha became absorbed in plans for reprisals

in England. Something of the sort had been suggested by Lynch and other country officers as a means of countering the wholesale wanton destruction wrought by the Black and Tans and Auxiliaries, but Brugha carried it a step further. His proposals included the bombing and machine-gunning of civilian crowds in theatres and cinemas, which was what the Black and Tans themselves did at Croke Park a few weeks later. Collins, however, threw up his hands in horror at the very idea.

'You'll get none of my men for that,' he snapped.

'I want none of your men, Mr. Collins,' said Brugha suavely.

The cabinet rejected the plans without question, but Brugha afterwards pursued Collins with unrelenting hatred, and Stack seconded him as though from the position of impartial observer. The cabinet meetings began to degenerate into quarrels between them and Collins. Outside the cabinet there was no pretence of impartiality. Stack had joined a small anti-Collins faction which consisted partly of women, whose principal grievance against Collins was his bad manners. He would no longer allow Collins to be referred to as the 'Big Fellow', proof enough that the origin of the nickname had been forgotten.

CHAPTER XI

BLOODY SUNDAY

THE English did not wish to declare a state of war, and the fight, as I have already said, had become one between two Secret Services. Though the Volunteers ambushed lorries and attacked barracks, and the military instituted vast roundups, thousands of men on both sides never had a shot fired in anger at them; the real fighters were postmen, telephone operators, hotel porters, cipher experts; the only real weapon, the revolver.

119

MacSwiney, the last of the romantics, lay in prison, wasting away in silent protest, when the first of the realists, Breen and Treacy, were captured by British Intelligence officers in Professor Carolan's. They shot their way out, killing two of the assassins. Collins had Breen, who was badly wounded, removed to a private room in the Mater Hospital. A few days later it was surrounded by a huge force of soldiers and police. Collins then took the amazing step of ordering out the whole Squad to make a fight for Breen.

O'Reilly took the order to Dick MacKee at a men's outfitting shop in Talbot Street. MacKee with a shrug said Collins was mad but sent O'Reilly to get the men from Parnell Square. He and Clancy set off, leaving Treacy to follow. They had only turned into O'Connell Street when the lorries dashed up—a telephone message had reached the Castle from premises across the road. Treacy walked out coolly, and an Intelligence officer grappled with him; the soldiers in the lorry let loose a machine gun, and a moment later the two bodies were lying together on the footpath, Treacy's Russian boots emerging from his long pants.

Breen escaped attention, but Collins, downcast over Treacy's fate, saw to his safety. He admired Breen, 'the man who began the war,' but indeed he admired every man who used his gun wisely or otherwise. He treated his own exploits lightly (we probably know only a fraction of them), but he read the dispatches of Hales or MacEoin with schoolboy excitement, talking to himself, laughing, thumping the table, and crying, 'Those are the fellows who should get the guns.' Their exploits became part of his imagination, like those of Michael Dwyer or Kelly of Killann, which had fired his fancy as a boy; he enjoyed telling the whole story of their fights, and told it with such vividness and enthusiasm that he seemed to have been an eyewitness. He loved meeting them and seemed a different man when they were there.

But his admiration for courage was equalled by his sensitiveness to pain, and there was a brooding horror in his voice as he told of some new devilry of the Secret Service, tears of impotent rage standing in his eyes, and his knuckles white.

Others could, and did, wisely forget what happened to a man when once the gates of an English barracks shut upon them until the moment when a poster told them he had died that morning, but Collins almost lived with them. Friendly guards, warders, doctors, chaplains, solicitors, were all in touch with him; he made it his business to trace a man's progress from the barracks to the torture room, from the torture room to the court martial where the judges sat with revolvers at their elbows, from the court martial to the condemned cell, from the condemned cell to the scaffold; he received messages from them and looked after their anguished mothers and wives. He carried a plan of each prison in his mind. His plans to rescue prisoners were often reckless; there were times when he seemed almost insane; certainly, with that feminine delicacy of emotion which is such a marked feature of his character, he must often have run close to the border line of sanity. Then his will would take control, and the blinding emotion was transformed into plans, so minute, logical, almost meticulous, that one would have said they were the work of a different being, a man who was all mind.

One can only regret that on paper it is Collins the conqueror who has survived. Of the agony of spirit he went through from this time practically until his death we have little record and can only guess it from some blundering phrase in a clear, businesslike letter, paragraphed, numbered and filed, or from some revealing phrase of one of his associates.

First there was the arrest and torture of Tom Hales, an old friend of his. Hale's companion went mad. Collins was like a lost soul. He sent one of his men to England with some of the Cork Intelligence men to try and kill the torturer. Yet when Collins writes to Griffith, it is to inquire if there was any insanity in the family of the man who had gone mad. He made preliminary inquiries with the hope of rescuing Hales.

Hard on that came another horror. Kevin Barry, a young student, was taken in action. His gallantry under the cruellest ill treatment thrilled Collins as it thrilled all Ireland. His captors taunted him with the powerlessness of Collins.

'What can your leaders do for you now?' they asked.

121

'They can do nothing for me,' he answered, 'but I can die for them.'

There began again that patient elaboration of plans. This time they were on a gigantic scale. He proposed to·blow the whole side wall of the prison away; some of the men were detailed to hold off the guard and others to fight their way through to young Barry's cell. The time chosen was the evening before the execution. A little crowd was waiting in Devlin's to hear the results. They knew, if the plan succeeded, Collins would enter like a whirlwind and the night would end in a characteristic debauch of violence. They started as they heard his step at the door and then the tramp, tramp on the stair; not Collins' usual confident bound, six stairs at a time, but the tread of a beaten man. He came in, his face drawn with agony, his long lock of hair drooping.

'The poor kid!' they heard him mutter as he strode across the room.

As the Volunteers had been about to launch their attack a crowd of women gathered to say the rosary outside the jail gates; it grew to such dimensions that the Castle was informed and armoured cars and reinforcements were rushed to the prison.

It was becoming obvious if Ireland did not have her Bloody Sunday England would have hers.

For six months Collins had been watching the procedure of the English Secret Service as it spied and murdered. From their first appearance on the Irish scene he had been gathering information about them. They had murders galore to their credit. They had murdered Lynch in the Exchange Hotel. One of the murderers, a masochistic savage, in one of his periodical fits of repentance blurted out the whole story to one of Collins' Intelligence officers. He mentioned other names; Collins got in touch with them and found them living as private citizens in respectable houses. He tapped their correspondence, had the contents of their wastepaper baskets examined, got duplicate keys made for their rooms. He waited until they became really dangerous. Aimes and Bennet, the leaders of the gang, caught Frank Thornton a short time before Bloody Sunday when he was actually keeping them under observation. After ten days he was allowed to go; it was only two days later that they realised whom they had let slip. The same thing occurred with Tobin and Cullen; a week before Bloody Sunday they were trapped in Vaughan's Hotel by Aimes and Bennet and put through a fierce examination. And again, a few days too late, the British found out who the two men were. It boded ill for any of Collins' men who fell into their hands now.

Saturday was a very busy day for Collins and his men. The lists had to be checked; another Secret Service man had been discovered and his name added; provision had to be made for one whole area which had failed. On Saturday night some of Collins Intelligence officers met and discussed it in the Gaiety Theatre. Near them sat some of the British Intelligence officers. Collins attended a meeting of officers in Vaughan's Hotel. A little after half-past ten Christy Harte, the porter, interrupted them. A British Secret Service man staying in the hotel had just gone out and returned. 'All right, Christy,' replied Collins. He and the others had only left the hotel when a British raiding party arrived. When the little group of leaders broke up that night it was with grim emotions. Brugha and Mulcahy went off to spend a sleepless night, Brugha tiptoeing about the room in his stockings with his revolver drawn, waiting for a raid that never came. MacKee and Clancy went off together to a usual haunt of theirs in Gloucester Street. Collins, Tobin and O'Sullivan were almost captured as they emerged from the hotel and ran into the raiders. They bolted into a hall, where they spent an uneasy night under the skylight, with a table and chair to take the place of a ladder.

Sunday morning dawned bright and cold. A little while after eight o'clock groups of men began to converge upon hotels, blocks of flats, and boarding houses in the centre of Dublin. A discreet knock and they were admitted. Then a revolver was brandished in the servant's face, a guard was placed in the hall, and the men began to mount the stairs on tiptoe. Another discreet knock and a bedroom door opened and revealed a young man in pyjamas, his face still flushed with

123

sleep. Seeing the tense faces and drawn revolvers, he threw up his hands and was pushed out of the room. In another room the men had forced their way in before the sleeper sprang up with a hand on his pistol. A shot broke the silence which had fallen since the bells of the city had ceased to call for nine-o'clock Mass; a young head fell back upon the pillow, and a red streak spread about it. The portrait of a girl continued to smile from the dressing table. The murderer of Lynch had the same end he had given his victim; he had only time to see the door burst in and the revolvers levelled.... Another died half way through the window with the revolvers barking over his screaming wife's shoulder.... A fusillade in the street; an officer's servant had escaped and was firing back at the house with a .22 pistol. The Auxiliaries began to close in; the men were surrounded. They rushed down the stairs and shot their way out the back, all but one, Teeling, who fell wounded in the garden, his gun by his side.

The plan had so far miscarried that half the spies and almost all the papers had escaped. A whole batch of Secret Service men had not even been attacked. But if every spy and tout in Ireland had been massacred the consternation in Dublin Castle could not have been greater; even at this stage they were like the people who walked in darkness: and the sound of the shots had scarcely given place to the mad screaming of Lancia cars when cabs began to drive up to the gate of Dublin Castle to disgorge pale-faced men and sobbing women with their baggage thrown anyhow inside.

At nine Collins was sitting in Devlin's, waiting for O'Reilly's report on the battle. O'Reilly cycled from post to post, collecting reports. Already there was an evil feeling in the sun-bright streets. The maddened Auxiliaries sprang from their lorries at every street corner and lashed out at the terrified passers-by. Tobin and Cullen escaped by the skin of their teeth. When O'Reilly arrived Collins listened, white and defiant, with no expression of pleasure.

'Any casualties?'

O'Reilly, who had not yet had a report from the party which had lost Teeling, said not.

'There'll be no hurling match today,' said Collins grimly. 'Go down to —— and tell him to call it off.'

O'Reilly cycled off to warn an official of the Gaelic Athletic Association, but it was too late. Even if the match were not played crowds would be certain to gather. Again Collins asked where were MacKee and Clancy. It was strange that they showed no curiosity about the operation they had planned. O'Reilly was sent to find them.

He cycled towards the district in which they usually passed the night. On his way he met one of Collins' Intelligence officers, and they strolled along together. In the side streets the city still preserved its Sabbath calm. After a few minutes a lad came towards them.

'Are you looking for MacKee and Clancy?'

'We are.'

'They were captured last night. I was told to send a message to Collins.'

Stupefied by the news, O'Reilly returned to Devlin's. Collins flared up at him, half rising from behind a table, his hands on the edge of it, his head forward—a favourite posture.

'Well, where are they?'

'They were captured last night.'

'Good God!' Collins gazed before him in a dazed way and sank back into his chair. 'We're finished now. It's all up.'

The little crowd in the room watched him with fascination. He began to stride up and down, digging in his heels, as his way was when perturbed.

'Get me MacNamara,' he snapped at last.

O'Reilly went out and searched vainly in the neighbourhood of the Castle. MacNamara himself arrived in Devlin's a few moments later. He had heard that two men had been removed to Bridewell, and that they answered the description of Mac-Kee and Clancy. There was still a faint hope. Half mad with anxiety, Collins ordered him and Neligan to search the Bridewell for them, while the Squad men available stood ready to fight their way in. After a while the two men came back crestfallen. MacKee and Clancy were in Dublin Castle.

The sense of impending evil deepened with every hour.

Auxiliaries and soldiers surrounded the athletic grounds at Croke Park and machine-gunned the defenceless crowd, the majority of whom were even yet unaware of what had really happened that morning. A player lay dead upon the field, and everywhere the dead and dying lay about in scores. The detectives hurried to Collins with the story that MacKee and Clancy with an inoffensive lad called Clune had been tortured and shot in the guardroom of the Castle. As the bodies were loaded on to a lorry at twilight, they had seen the torturer flashing his lamp on the bodies and battering the dead faces in a maniacal fury. Terrible stories were circulated about their fate. Collins continued to repeat that it was over. Even his friends, who knew his intense loyalty and the way he reacted to suffering, were alarmed. It was as though he no longer thought of anything else. One colleague describes him, swaying to and fro with anguish as he recounted the sufferings of the dead men afresh, so vividly one could feel he was living it through, and at each swing of his body his revolver tapped against the leg of the table.

When the bodies of the murdered men were handed over to their relatives and brought to the Pro-Cathedral, Collins insisted that he and their other friends must attend and dress the dead men in their officers' uniforms. To some of them it sounded like suicide. A few refused to come, and Collins, enraged, lashed out at them. His immediate followers, though they took it to be the last thing they were likely to do for him, agreed. Uniforms were procured, and in the dark winter evening he and the others cycled up to the Pro-Cathedral gate through a knot of gaping detectives and spies. The three coffins lay in the little mortuary chapel. It was a macabre scene. In the chapel there were perhaps twenty people who spoke in whispers, expecting every moment the rush of maddened Auxiliaries. The candles flickered in the wind. Outside, the streets were cold, dreary, and full of mist. Collins stood in silence, watching, while the coffins were opened to reveal the swollen and blackened faces of his friends. A sob went up from those around as the doctors bent over them. Even in death the mouths were drawn up in a snarl of pain. The doctors

126

examined the bodies swiftly while the onlookers helped to turn them. Mercifully, things were not so bad as had been said. Except for the gaping holes of bullets fired point-blank there were only the marks of rifle butts and bayonets. The three men were dressed in their officers' uniforms, and, because the clergy would not permit the battered faces to be left bare to the eyes of the crowd, the coffins were nailed down for the last time. To everyone it was quite plain from Collins' demeanour that he was now utterly indifferent to what might happen to him. No one ever had a more loyal friend, but so many of his friends were gone; and those who were left could only look forward to a fate like this.

When the sinister ceremony was over, Collins merely mounted his bicycle and rode off scowling through the detectives. Next morning he went off once more to the Pro-Cathedral for the Requiem Mass. There was the same tiny crowd, the same feeling in everyone of Collins' utter recklessness, the tragic indifference that had fallen on him.

That fatalistic gloom hung over him, his friends agree, a long time, but, whatever shadow may have fallen upon him in moments of relaxation, there was no emotion which could stand up long to that immense will power. This emotion, too, the greatest perhaps he had yet known, was ground into action, leaving him as carefree as before and with even more of that magic which was beginning to surround him. That week after Bloody Sunday was so terrible that people did not dare to venture out. Collins cycled round as coolly as ever. When no one could be found to receive messages from the detectives, he went himself. A week after Bloody Sunday he was thrilled by the ambush at Kilmichael in which a small column which included his brother Sean, had wiped up a party of Auxiliaries. He burst in once more like a whirlwind, sweeping hats, caps and coats off hallstands in his glee and proclaiming in triumphant tones that Cork could show them how to fight.

For several Sundays the Squad waited for the remaining political detectives outside the church where they heard Mass, and desisted only when a newspaper boy shouted 'Hi, gentlemen, ye're late again.' A week or two later Ryan, the informer who had given away MacKee and Clancy, was riddled.

It took a lot to knock Collins out.

CHAPTER XII

DE VALERA RETURNS

HEADQUARTERS and cabinet alike had refused to listen to Brugha's plea for bloody reprisals in England, but were forced to agree to some sort of campaign; country officers had been demanding it as the only measure which would halt the destruction being wrought at home. Rory O'Connor was sent across to organise it. The result was to create chaos in Collins' English organisation. Up to this, things had been run, and very efficiently run, by the small group of I.R.B. men under his immediate control. Now, for mass operations, companies of volunteers were necessary. O'Connor addressed assembled recruits in a smoky cellar under Scotland Road and warned them that they must consider themselves in the front line henceforth. To make matters worse, Kerr and Lanigan of Liverpool were arrested. At the same time as the Kilmichael ambush the Volunteers demolished rows of warehouses in Liverpool, the value of which ran into fabulous sums.

Collins, however, succeeded in restoring communications, and, desperately hampered as it was, the work of arms purchases and communications went on.

At the end of November 1920 Griffith was arrested, and for some weeks Collins was in fact acting president of Dail Eireann.

It was at this time Lloyd George showed the first signs of caving in. He began to send out feelers for negotiations. He did so in a fashion calculated to produce the maximum of distrust and obstinacy. He would negotiate, he wouldn't negotiate; he would insist on surrender, he would parley with the Republicans as equals; he would deal with Collins, Collins must be handed over. One day he was all conciliation; next, stung by some trifling remark or petty engagement, he was all fire and fury again. Then once more he sent for some prominent Irishman like Æ. From the beginning Collins did not trust him. He had the Conservative Irishman's dislike of all Liberal and labour politicians. Nor did he allow the statement that his personal position was holding up negotiations to go unchallenged. He issued a fiery reply. 'No person in Ireland or anywhere else had authority to use my name. My personal safety does not count as a factor in the question of Ireland's right. I thank no one for refraining from murdering me.' Lloyd George's intermediary, the Archbishop of Perth, found some suspicious-looking characters about his house, waiting for the expected visit from Collins. At last the two men were allowed to meet in peace, but having been put off once or twice, Collins decided that Lloyd George was only temporising.

But Lloyd George was as much in earnest as it was possible for him to be. He was merely swayed by every wind that blew, and the wind just then was blowing particularly hard from over the North Atlantic. Then a light breeze rose from among the moderate Sinn Feiners. Father O'Flanagan offered to negotiate with Lloyd George direct. Another Sinn Feiner, Sweetman, also spoke; an old follower of Griffiths, he was pacifist on principle. A small group of Parliamentarians in Galway passed a resolution which completed the picture of a nation beaten to its knees. And there was a considerable amount of truth in the picture, as Volunteer headquarters knew to its cost. One county council was prepared to rat from its allegiance to Dail Eireann and was restrained only by some weighty arguments in the form of Webley revolvers.

Lloyd George was in ecstasy. He tapped the papers before him and cried exultantly, 'We have those fellows beaten!' Dublin Castle was in ecstasy too. Father O'Flanagan's intervention had given it a new lease of life. All through December the negotiations dragged on, only to collapse upon Lloyd George's final resolution that the Volunteers must first surrender their arms.

Meanwhile de Valera, who had been almost cut off from knowledge of events at home and probably feared a total collapse of the revolutionary movement, hastened back to Ireland. Collins was delighted at the prospect of his return. He had foreseen the necessity and made the arrangements. The *Lapland* had been transferred to the Hamburg route, so he had made O'Neill and Downes sign on for the *Celtic*. They squared the bos'n. Meanwhile Liverpool had been fired, and a discarded seaman's card of O'Neill's, in which he figured as John Murphy, had come into the possession of the police. On the twentieth of December 1920, when the *Lapland* arrived, they were waiting to interview the missing sailors. This was something Collins had not anticipated, but the friendly bos'n whipped de Valera to a place of safety while the detectives searched the ship.

It was Christmas Eve morning when de Valera reached Dublin. Collins was up at five to welcome him. He had high hopes that de Valera's intervention would put an end to the row between himself and the Stack–Brugha group. They met at a house in Merrion Square. It was eighteen months since they had parted, the Long Fellow and the Big Fellow. For each of them those eighteen months had been packed with incident. De Valera had been treated like a king; Collins like an escaped convict. One by one members of the cabinet saw him.

But it was Christmas, which to a man of Collins' temperament was sacred to festivity. His Christmases were always Dickensian, with plenty of drink, good food, relaxed discipline and wholesome good humour. It was a busy time for O'Reilly. There were the seamen, each of whom got a five-pound note and, if they were free, an invitation to meet him in a pub. There were presents to be purchased for the scores of people who had helped him during the year: the women who had sheltered him, the detectives who had given him information —all those not actually part of the movement whose sympathy made so much difference. Each of the presents went out with a little note which the recipient would not dare to treasure. Then, so far as possible, he paid each of his friends a short visit, as though to show what he was like off the job.

After lunch O'Reilly went off on his round of present bearing. Collins had had an early start and a busy day, and was hungry. Rather than give Mrs. Devlin the trouble of preparing food, he, O'Connor, O'Sullivan, Tobin and Cullen decided to dine in town. It was four o'clock and only a hundred yards to the Gresham Hotel. The Gresham's private rooms were booked, so they sat in the big dining room and ordered a meal with wine. They were only halfway through it when a waiter appeared at Collins' elbow.

'You might like to know, sir,' he said in a discreet whisper, 'the Auxiliaries are in the hall.'

They had two minutes in which to prepare before the Auxiliaries burst in upon them, brandishing revolvers and rifles. They rose with their hands in the air. As a preliminary the Auxiliaries searched them.

'Eh, what's this?' asked the man who was searching Collins, and from his hip-pocket produced a bottle of whiskey.

'Stop!' said Collins good-humouredly. 'That's a present for the landlady.'

He gave his name as John Grace. He must be the only revolutionary on record who did not say his name was Smith. The famous notebook was examined but the only word the Auxiliary officer could identify was one which he declared was 'rifles' and which Collins indignantly declared was 'refills'.

When this hitch was got over, he made an excuse and withdrew to the lavatory under escort. O'Connor took up the whiskey he had left behind and invited the Auxiliaries to share it. A corkscrew was produced and another of the guests ordered a second bottle. Noticing his chief so long away, and filled, as they were all filled, with alarm only for his safety, Tobin made a similar excuse. To his consternation he found the officer holding Collins back over a wash basin where the light was most brilliant; teasing his hair about with one hand while in the other he held a photograph of the very man he was examining. The photograph was a bad one, but not so bad that recognition was impossible. To his immense relief the officer released Collins, and the two of them returned to the dining

131

room. 'Be ready to make a rush for it,' Collins whispered.

But it was unnecessary. The atmosphere in the dining room had changed from distrust to maudlin pleasantry. The Auxiliaries departed, leaving five men almost crazy with relief. They drank whiskey in neat tumblersful, but it seemed as if nothing could quiet their nerves. They continued to celebrate in Vaughan's Hotel. In a comparatively brief space of time they were drunk and indulging in horseplay, oblivious of their danger. It was the only occasion on which most of those present saw Collins drunk. O'Hegarty, who had missed the dinner party at the Gresham, was begging them to come away before Vaughan's was also raided. They ignored him.

They finally drove to Mrs. O'Donovan's in a car and bundled themselves into bed. It was a Christmas none of them was likely to forget.

It is hard to say which was the more bewildered at de Valera's return, he or the little group he had left behind. Each had grown; each, existing in an equally artificial atmosphere, had viewed the other through a haze of sentiment; and now the sentiment was being rudely dissipated.

De Valera interviewed his cabinet and headquarters, man by man, inquired minutely into the military position, and told of his American experiences, which began to get on Collins' nerves. He had come home with new plans. On the one hand the war must be made to slacken off, so far as concerned the shooting of policemen and the minor ambushing of soldiers—this in order to save the civilian population from the savage reprisals with which those activities were associated; on the other, it must be pursued by huge bodies of men facing the enemy in pitched battles which would last for days. Collins, who knew the exact amount of labour it involved to equip one column of sixteen men, and how even these were constantly being forced into inactivity for lack of a few rounds of rifle ammunition, tried to disillusion him.

The Dail was summoned to meet de Valera, but at the last moment, acting on the advice of Brugha, he did not turn up. Neither did Brugha; and Collins, to save his chief's face, was also compelled to absent himself. The Dail was properly infuriated, and whatever effect de Valera might have hoped to have at first, it was certain he would have none now. A second meeting was hurriedly summoned. It was held in Walter Cole's house. It reflected the changed conditions. At a table outside the door sat a group of Collins' men, playing cards and smoking, their revolvers beside them. He commented grimly that it looked like a scene from a cowboy film. The delegates were not long in informing de Valera that if he wished to lead them. it could only be in a fight. They took the opportunity of lashing out at Sweetman, Roche and O'Flanagan, and Collins indulged in a characteristic outburst in which he pointed out that Cork, which had fought best, had suffered least, and Galway, which had fought lest, had suffered most.

Collins was certainly disillusioned. When de Valera began once more to describe the state in which he had paraded America, he ground out a remark to the effect that if he had been there he would have seen that no such waste occurred. On another occasion: 'Oh, I have it off by heart!' He made no real attempt to impress de Valera and at the first cabinet meeting held after his return put in an appearance in what was for him a queer humour—almost melancholy. He created amusement among his friends by adopting a defeatist attitude on a proposal to prohibit the English census and declared that the English would beat them on it.

By February Collins and Mulcahy had apparently given de Valera up as a bad job. After O'Malley's interview with de Valera Collins asked, 'What did you think of the interview?' 'He did not know much about the Army in the South,' replied O'Malley.

'Both laughed as if amused. Collins mentioned some of the questions the President had asked; they laughed again. I felt uncomfortable.'*

De Valera had come home with yet another proposal. Collins must go to America. There is no reason whatever to suppose that the suggestion was dictated by jealousy. In view of de Valera's opinion that the fight should slacken off, it was only natural that the man who was looked on as head of the

* O'Malley: *On Another Man's Wound.*

extremists should be got out of the way.

In fact the proposal had been made before, on the occasion of the American split, the idea being to make Collins take a rest; but this time Collins was firmly convinced that it had originated with Brugha and Stack, and with no other idea than to get rid of him. It created consternation among the officers. Several talked of sending in their resignation. There would certainly have been a serious breakup within the army, and it is unlikely that the political movement would have escaped. But Collins put his foot down at last. 'The Long Whoor won't get rid of me as easy as that,' he said.

This was a bad beginning to de Valera's intervention in the Brugha–Collins quarrel, and it is hard to see exactly what he did to curb it that would not have been better undone. By assuming the position of unprejudiced observer and electing to hold the balance between them, he really kept them divided. Of course he increased his own prestige. The contending groups were bound to bid for his support. Brugha and Stack felt he favoured them. Collins felt he favoured him; and as will be shown, the normal division of opinion which was bound to result from the signing of the Treaty was immensely complicated by the fact that instead of two parties there were three—diehards, moderates and de Valera.

Collins had troubles enough without that. On New Year's Eve Eileen MacGrane's flat was raided and a heap of Collins' old files was captured. It included all the Castle documents and those of the Detective Division, as well as the headquarters daybook which he had carried off from Brunswick Street and which had escaped the attention of the Auxiliaries during the raid on Smith's a few days before. It was the weakness of Collins' method of work. He hated to part with files, even when they had ceased to be useful, and never took sufficient precautions to ensure that the people referred to would not be identified—though the Intelligence Department was now using numbers, and he had Batt O'Connor constructing clever hiding places for its papers. This was the first intimation the Castle received of the effectiveness of Collins' methods, and they began upon the lengthy process of elimination which resulted in Broy's arrest.

On the same night Christy Harte, the porter at Vaughan's Hotel, was arrested. Tired of threatening Harte, the Secret Service men at the Castle tried a new dodge. After being held for five days he was brought into a long room, curtained at one end. The lights went out and a voice pealed out at Harte from the darkness. It recounted suavely the grip which the British now had on the rebel organisation; Griffith and the rest had been captured; there remained only Collins. Harte was a poor man; £5,000 would be placed to his credit at the bank and a free passage given him to any country he chose if only he would give Collins away. But he didn't know Collins, Harte protested. Well, the voice went on imperturbably, if he got to know Collins, all he had to do was ring Dublin Castle, Extension 28, and say, 'The portmanteau is now ready.'

Collins was having a succession of narrow shaves which would have broken the nerve of any other man. On one occasion the military raided a house at Donnybrook. The officer, with a sheet of paper in his hand, was rummaging among a lot of love letters when the girl to whom they were addressed protested. The officer apologised, and in his haste and confusion left behind him the sheet of paper he was carrying with him. It contained the list of houses he had been ordered to raid. On noticing his loss, he rang up Dublin Castle but they refused to repeat instructions over the telephone. After he had gone the girl picked up the list and saw that the only address still unraided was 23 Brendan Road. Next morning she passed on the slip of paper to Batt O'Connor, who saw to his consternation that it was the very house where Collins had spent the night.

On another occasion he was leaving Vaughan's Hotel with O'Sullivan and O'Hegarty to sleep at the Thousand Gallons (as he called the distillery where he sometimes hid) when they found themselves caught near a church in the city. They rushed for cover to the shadow of the buttresses, each taking advantage of the narrow pile of stone, and spent the night there, their shoulders pressed back into the damp corner. A few yards away a sentry strode up and down, clashing the butt

135

of his rifle upon the flagstones. They dared not speak, and when dawn was creeping into the sky they had to resist the cough which shook them from the contact of their shoulders with the damp stone.

Twice he was held up in a car with important papers on him. On the first occasion he simply strode up to the officer in charge of the search party and chatted merrily with him while the car and its other occupants were searched. On the second occasion he was returning to town after a consultation with Neligan, Broy and MacNamara at Gay's house in Clontarf. At Newcomen Bridge they were halted by a patrol of soldiers. It was fortunate for Collins that the detectives were with him. When they showed their passes the military informed them that an ambush had just taken place near the bridge. The officer advised them not to drive forward because the Sinn Feiners were still there. They thanked him for the information, Broy called to Collins, who had jumped out, ready for fight, 'Step in, Sergeant!' and they drove off in safety. Once he was searched, when he had £16,000 of Republican funds on him, but the Auxiliaries who searched him were too drunk to discover it.

What saved him, as it saved so many others of the time, was the instinct for danger. This was not mere nervousness; it came of an iron control over the nerves. Only when one had that iron control did one become aware of coincidence, warning whispers, a sense of being protected from outside. Little unrelated things comforted, disturbed. Collins slept better when he could hear the stirring of horses in the stable near Devlin's; he took fright after passing one night in a strange house because the birds did not sing outside his window at dawn.

He leaned upon that sense of protection, played with it. At curfew time he might be seen in Lindsay Road, outside the house where O'Hegarty and O'Sullivan stayed, calling them back with mock earnestness while the lorries could be heard tearing up towards them.

One night, long after curfew, he climbed the wall between the house where he was staying and Smith's, where Joe

O'Reilly was. He brought his bicycle with him and left it in the yard. Only after a rough-and-tumble did he announce his intention. He wanted to pay a call on his sister, whom he had failed to see during the day! They thought him mad, but he grew angrier and more insistent. O'Reilly, giving himself up for lost, got out his bicycle, and the two men rode off through the streets which were as silent as the grave and utterly deserted, their bicycle lamps the only illumination. The call over, they returned as they had come, in safety!

On another occasion Lindsay Road was filled with Auxiliaries and soldiers. Collins looked out to see them knocking at Smith's—by some amazing chance O'Reilly had failed to get there that night. He knew he had left the old daybook which he had pinched from detective headquarters there, and waited to see the result. Next morning, when Miss Smith was sweeping out the traces of the Auxiliaries' presence, the door of the near-by house opened and Collins appeared, pushing his bicycle and grinning delightedly. She waited for some inquiry about her ordeal. Instead, she was greeted with a laugh and a broad jest.

Next time it was Collins who was delayed and O'Reilly who arrived. In the morning he woke up to find the whole road cut off by barbed wire. While the officer was searching another house, he strode out and braved the sentry with the statement that he was employed at Dublin Castle. He was allowed to pass, though the whole area was invested for days. Yet Collins could still find time for a thousand kindnesses. On the day of the Lindsay Road raid a spy was shot in Dublin. Pakenham tells the story of what followed. His wife, believing he had been killed by the British, asked for assistance for herself and her child from Volunteer sources. When the matter was reported to Collins he ordered instantly that she should get assistance and that nothing should be said to the innocent child which would suggest that her father had died a traitor's death.

It was a wild existence, its wildness heightened by the dullness of everyday life which went on about it, by sharp contrasts which drew nervous laughter from Collins with his

137

keen sense of comedy. One Sunday morning Hurley rushed down to Devlin's with news that Mulcahy and O'Hegarty had been trapped in a house in Parnell Square. 'I'll get Tobin and some of the boys, and we won't be long getting them away,' said Collins, and whistling he rushed upstairs for his gun. As he and a companion strode quickly up the square they met Mulcahy and O'Hegarty coming towards them. 'Can't ye bloody children look after yeerselves yet?' said Collins with a grin. 'What can I do for ye now?' The four went down O'Connell Street together. It was all peaceful with a Sunday-morning calm. A policeman, standing against a shop window, lowered his eyes discreetly as they approached. But as they came abreast of him he raised his head. 'Good morrrning, boys,' he boomed sheepishly. Collins exploded in a chuckle. 'The comic war!' he said with a toss of his head.

There was a party thrown by a returned Irish–American which was attended by the whole of G.H.Q., Intelligence Staff and detectives. It was a lavish spread. The table was decorated with the initials 'I.R.A.' in the green and gold of apples and oranges. 'What does it feel like to be a great man?' a lady asked breathlessly of Collins. 'How do I know?' he growled and in his embarrassment began to pelt the other guests with nuts.

Then came Broy's arrest. Fortunately he was able to show that another beside himself might be responsible, and before the British could locate the man, who was then living in England, Collins had him packed out of the country. This looked so much like a confession of guilt on his part that Broy, though detained, was allowed to live. There is no doubt what his fate would have been had the charges against him been proved.

Then MacNamara was dismissed. With him it was also doubt rather than conviction. He was shrewd enough to simulate indignation, and his chief, perturbed at the dismissal of so excellent a man, expressed his deep regret.

'It's a conspiracy!' declared MacNamara vehemently.

'No, MacNamara, merely a mistake, I assure you! Merely a mistake!'

Neligan was now alone in the Castle—fortunately he had

shammed a feud with Broy during their association, but at any rate the day of the Detective Division was over. Of all the daring features of a daring time there are few to equal the achievement of these three men.

CHAPTER XIII

TRUCE

In his fight with Collins Brugha had a weapon to hand in Mellowes, who had just returned from America and been appointed Director of Purchases—the job Collins had been carrying on for years as a side line. The transference of accounts provided a grand excuse for a quarrel. Brugha demanded detailed statements of the expenditure to date. Now Collins had been administering two sources of revenue—the public money voted by Dail Eireann and the secret funds of the Republican Brotherhood. He had tried to keep these moneys separate, but that was rarely possible, and the accounts also overlapped. This was sufficient to irritate Brugha, even if there had been no discrepancies. But there were. It was impossible that money should not have been lost or misappropriated. If you give a sailor on his way to Hamburg £20 to purchase revolvers he may or may not return with them, and money, thousands of pounds of it, was always out in this way on the off-chance of a likely deal. It was handled by men unaccustomed to bookkeeping on the grand scale, in the payment of rascally non-commissioned officers, fences, crooks and every type of shady character. The Glasgow arms transactions of which Mellows and Brugha complained were the largest carried out by Collins' men; a quotation or two from the files may show the conditions under which they worked.

'Our new channels are —— Bks., —— Bks., H. and S., in —— we are in direct touch with the sergeant in the machine-gun store and he is extra, he is only waiting now to get his right man on sentry for to start working for us, we are expecting the word from him at any time, and may perhaps get up to ten or more machine guns from him, the job he is on now is squaring the sentries, of course we will have to pay for that work. . . .'

And again:

'We brought off a deal on 22nd Wed. with two soldiers out of Hamilton Barracks for 40 German rifles and bayonets. I had 30 of the boys and a Taxi on the job at 1 a.m. Thurs. everything went fine, we got them over the wall and away in about 20 minutes, we fixed up for £60 but paid £40 and kept remainder until after we inspect them.'

It was the opinion of the staff that the money could not possibly have been more scrupulously used; the accounts—very full and detailed ones—are as well vouched as those of most private businesses; but Brugha was not satisfied. On one occasion he told his friends that Collins, in tears, had confessed that he had diverted government money to assist a relative; which, as anyone who has handled even a petty cash account will realise, might mean anything or nothing. Everybody in charge of money is liable to make use of it at some time: the question is, does he falsify his accounts to conceal it?

Stack, who certainly knew better, adopted a judicial air—it must have been a pleasant change for him to sit in judgment on Collins—and said the charges were grave. Mellowes, who for a short time sided with Brugha, did likewise. There were furious scenes, and Collins was bitterly hurt at the imputation of dishonesty. Mulcahy prepared an elaborate system of accounting to meet the wishes of his tetchy chief. Brugha replied magniloquently, 'So long as the generally accepted laws of accountancy are not deviated from I am satisfied.' Even the grave Mulcahy smiled. But Brugha could not long contain his distrust of Collins, and the next paragraph shows that it wasn't bookkeeping that concerned him. 'No one on this side should intermeddle with the work of the department without the

140

authority of the Director of Purchases or Quartermaster General.'

While the generally accepted laws of accountancy were being observed, men were dying for lack of the few rounds of ammunition with which to defend themselves. The Quartermaster General reported savagely that his men had seen 9,000 rounds of ammunition offered for sale in Glasgow, and had no money to purchase it; he hinted at what country Volunteers would do to them if they discovered that. Mellows replied that this might well be; at present he could not afford to have the accounts muddled by fresh disbursements!

Collins, with his passion for efficiency, was in despair. Writing in March to one of his lieutenants, he said, 'I am sorry that you are getting congested, but it is not my fault.... Some people here are entirely unreasonable. Even now things are far from square, and I am absolutely fed up.'

Brugha nagged on until an infuriated Headquarters Staff began to protest. Some months later Mulcahy went to de Valera and informed him that he must either control Brugha or accept his own resignation as Chief of Staff. De Valera agreed. 'Cathal is jealous of Mick,' he said. He did remonstrate with Brugha and Brugha broke down. 'I could not do wrong,' he said.

After this Brugha went back to his old mania—assassinating the British cabinet. Unknown to Collins he summoned some of the most daring Volunteer officers to Dublin. Among them was MacEoin whom he had chosen as leader of the London operations—MacEoin, who was lost outside his own countryside! Collins instructed MacEoin to see Mulcahy, who promptly sent him back. Dublin Castle, learning that MacEoin was on his way, ordered his arrest at Mullingar.

A police officer in Mullingar, who was one of Collins' men, tried to get some local volunteers to stop the train but failed. The station was surrounded and the passengers examined. MacEoin inevitably gave the name of Smith, and his friend the police officer affected to be satisfied. Then another man raised MacEoin's left arm and held it up to show the white pits dug in the flesh by sparks and said 'That is a blacksmith's arm.' MacEoin was handcuffed and marched towards the military barracks. Suddenly he hit out on either side with his elbows and dashed off down the main street. He dodged down a side street and into a patrol which shot him through the lung. Then he was savagely beaten with rifle butts, and in the day room, after the doctor had given him an hour to live, was stood against the wall, choking in his own blood while the Black and Tans hammered him. He was brought to Dublin roped to a stretcher with a revolver at his ear. Collins already had a column out to intercept the ambulance and escort but they entered Dublin by a back road.

Meanwhile, in the hope of avoiding direct negotiations with the Irish leaders, Lloyd George, frustrated in O'Flanagan, tackled local guerilla chiefs in the little group of counties known as the war zone, chiefly Cork and Kerry. These tactics, suggested by some busybody who believed that the Volunteers were sick of their leaders, were completely misunderstood and only stiffened resistance, so that the local go-betweens—politicians and solicitors who suddenly announced that they were in a position to offer terms, as from General Blank—received no hearing.

In April Collins had another close shave, one of dozens. His Intelligence Office at Mespil Road was raided. At a desk by the window the raiders found a brace of loaded revolvers. Fortunately for Collins they did not find the Intelligence files, though they almost tore the house to pieces; they were hidden under the window in one of the secret cupboards built for him by Batt O'Connor; if they had, Collins or no Collins, they could have paralysed the movement within a week or two.

But at least they hoped to get their man and occupied the house, clearing away all sign of their presence. At nine sharp Collins would ride up on his bicycle, push it round to the side, and stride in the back door in his fearless way—walking into their arms. Miss Hoey, who, with her invalid mother occupied the upstairs portion of the house, was arrested and taken to Dublin Castle. She, too, knew what was about to happen. She bluffed for all she was worth; the stakes were high. She was a journalist and the Press of the world would hear of their treatment of a woman. Late into the night she continued her fight for Collins' life. At last they gave in, and she was brought back to the house under escort.

The position seemed as hopeless as ever, but she persuaded her mother to sham collapse. There was a long struggle with the officer before he would consent to have a doctor called, but again she bluffed her way through and went off to find a woman doctor—escorted once more by policemen. The doctor, puzzled by Miss Hoey's statement that she had seen the old lady before, but vaguely suspecting that there was some urgent need of her, agreed to come. It was a strange party in a city of the dead: two women, one trying to tell the other of the trap, the other trying to understand and failing, while beside them walked two nervous Black and Tans who jumped at every sound.

When they reached the house Miss Hoey refused to allow her mother to be examined while the room was occupied by Black and Tans. Again there was a long argument; again she had her way. They withdrew on to the landing, and under a barrage of rattling bottles she revealed the extent of Collins' danger.

Even when the doctor had got free with the story and Collins' friends were informed, it was still questionable if he would escape the trap, as no one knew where he was staying. Scouts were finally posted at every road leading to the office, and Collins, Cullen and Miss Lyons, the typist, were all stopped in time.

MacEoin was now nearly well again, and Collins was busily planning to rescue him. It seemed an impossible task.

In George Vth Hospital he was taken downstairs to have the bullet removed from his lung, but as he reached the waiting room five innocent men—ex-British soldiers who had been shot to pieces by Auxiliaries—were brought in for immediate operation. As they came out of the operating theatre a British Intelligence Officer wrote down their rambling talk. MacEoin refused to be anaesthetised. The surgeons, realising what was happening, insisted on the removal of the Intelligence Officer and volunteered to remain by MacEoin's side till he came out of the ether, but he was taking no chances and underwent the operation with a local anaesthetic.

While he was still lying wounded in the military hospital he was visited by a priest who promptly proceeded to reproach him for his activity as an officer of the Volunteers. MacEoin, who felt he had enough to bear, considered this a bit thick. Suddenly he heard the priest's tirade interrupted by a whisper, 'I'm from the Big Fellow.' He cocked his ear. The room was cleared of guards. Then the priest hastily unfolded the plan. Like most of Collins' plans, it was extraordinarily daring. Next evening the guard would be changed in the ordinary way but a half-hour sooner. The guard would be Volunteers dressed in British uniform. Unfortunately, this plan was postponed for a few evenings. On the evening when it was finally due to take place MacEoin was transferred; an hour and a half too soon.

MacEoin had no notion where he was, merely that he was in a cell with a high barred window. After a short time he heard the familiar code knock on the heating pipes—two long and two short—signalling him that a message was on its way. Next day he was visited by a woman doctor who asked him if he was strong enough to move. MacEoin replied that he was, and, as she examined him, she slipped a piece of paper into his hand. It was a plan of the prison which showed him that he was on the ground floor of the prison hospital.

She was to visit him again on Wednesday of that week but failed to get in. On Thursday a friendly warder brought a parcel from her. It contained a hacksaw, a bottle of Three-in-One oil, a cake of soap, some clothes, and a watch. The plan was that at five minutes to seven on the following evening MacEoin would get through the cell window while the sentry was detained in conversation at the other side of the jail by a friendly warder, strike down the path towards a wicket gate, and inform the sentry that he was a warder going for a drink. Finally he would come to another gate, and on this, at the very stroke of seven, he was to knock. It would be opened for him by men of the Squad, who would bring a bicycle on which he would ride to Batt O'Connor's house in Donnybrook.

All night MacEoin worked, his task interrupted every ten minutes by the stride of the sentry on the pathway outside his window. In the early morning the bars were completely severed and the trace of the hacksaw filled with soap. But the night's labour had left him utterly exhausted. The prison doctor who visited him at noon found him with a temperature of 103. He turned upon the warder and abused him for having left the patient so long in a small, damp, groundfloor cell instead of having him shifted upstairs. The warder promised to see that the change was made without delay. MacEoin begged to be allowed to remain for just one more day, giving as excuse that his mother was coming to see him and would not be able to mount the stairs. But the doctor was adamant; his duty was to see that MacEoin got well and the sick man was shifted to the top of the building, above the Auxiliaries' quarters.

Another man would have lost heart. Not Collins though. He went to see Mrs. MacEoin to comfort her. 'Next time I come,' he promised 'I'll bring him with me. And it won't be long either.' He had got fresh inspiration from the report of the abattoir superintendent that an armoured car visited the abattoir each morning at an early hour, and that it might be possible to capture it. Dalton, whom he sent to spy out the ground, reported in similar terms. Collins had a revolver smuggled in to MacEoin in the prison hospital, warned him to try and reach the governor's office on the stroke of ten, and everything was ready for the great attempt.

Each morning the Squad waited in a position from which they could see a signal from Dalton, who occupied an upstairs room in a house overlooking the spot where the car halted. The essential thing was to get the whole crew outside, and that was a question of time. Each morning Collins visited the store from which the Squad departed, to see that everything was correct, even to the dungarees of the men who were to drive. When his hostess, an old lady, remonstrated with him for this foolhardiness, he nodded to O'Reilly who was just cycling off to early Mass from the house next door. 'I'm in no danger while I have the lad praying for me,' he said.

For days Dalton watched; then one morning he saw the whole crew emerge to smoke cigarettes in the morning sunshine. He raised the blind, and in a few moments the armoured car and its crew were surrounded. So far so good. The men who were to take the car pulled down the legs of the dungarees, which were hidden under their coats. A short distance away they stopped to pick up two men in the uniform of British officers, Emmet Dalton and Leonard. They had duplicate keys for the prison, with which Collins, with his amazing thoroughness, had supplied them.

At the prison gate Dalton produced Collins' demand for the body of MacEoin. It was an official government envelope. The prison gates opened and the car swept in. There were two inner gates, and under pretence of turning, the driver, Pat MacCrea, manoeuvred the car so that neither could be closed. Emmet Dalton and Leonard strode into the Governor's quarters as though they owned the prison.

The next step in the plan was that some women with parcels for prisoners should engage the warder at the main gate in an argument so as to keep it open. If that failed there were two men near with revolvers. It did fail. The warder was in surly mood; he proceeded to shut the gate in the women's faces, whereupon the two men drew revolvers and covered him.

The sentry in the courtyard, where the car had stopped, saw the drawn revolvers and fired at the two men, wounding one. One of the car's crew shot him down. But the alarm had been given and the machine gun on the roof began to spatter bullets all around. MacCrea ran the car forward and jammed the main gate.

Meanwhile the plan had failed in its most important particular. For several mornings in succession MacEoin had contrived with one excuse or another to be in the governor's office on the stroke of ten. This morning the guard was being changed, and he was told he must wait until the change was complete before being escorted to the office. Accordingly, Dalton and Leonard, faced by a suspicious governor, who wished to phone to Dublin Castle for confirmation of the written authority they bore, tied him up in his own office. As they rushed out to try their luck on the chief warder, firing began outside, and realising the game was up, they bolted for the car and made their escape under a hail of bullets. They had nothing to show for their pains but a couple of machine guns and some revolvers—these and the moral effect of their escapade, which was considerable.

One cannot avoid the feeling that in some extraordinary way Collins had succeeded as no one else before him had done in undermining a tyranny so that it was no longer substantial. His vast organisation had thrown it wide open, revealed exactly how it worked, like a great X-ray apparatus that made the task of government impossible.

To cheer him up there was Neligan's coup. With Broy in jail, MacNamara dismissed, and the bulk of the secret work in the hands of the Secret Service, Neligan felt himself useless. He suggested that he should try to join the Secret Service. Collins ridiculed the idea. Neligan persisted. He saw his police superior about it, and when asked his reason for seeking so dangerous a job, prudently said that he needed the money. That sounded convincing, so he was referred to the major in charge, who swore him in. He memorised the oath for Collins' benefit. It catalogued the punishment he might expect if he proved unfaithful. Then he was instructed in the signs, handclasps and passwords (on which Collins, it will be remembered, had been offered information, at a price).

Whereupon the Major, shaking him emotionally by the hand, said, 'Try to join the I.R.A., my boy. Try to join the I.R.A.!'

Collins, who was waiting in a pub round the corner to hear the result of the interview, enjoyed that touch of comedy.

A few weeks later came the burning of the Custom House, the biggest job yet tackled by the Volunteers. It was an attempt to paralyse English government completely by destroying all its revenue records, and in this it was successful, but it took a heavy toll of the Volunteers. Collins bemoaned the loss of so many of his best men.

Next day he had the narrowest shave of his career. He was expected at his office in Mary Street at the usual hour but

147

failed to put in an appearance. The typist and messenger commented upon the strangeness of this. Actually, Collins' instinct for danger was acute that day. He and O'Sullivan had lunched at Woolworth's, and a pretty waitress, attracted by Collins' appearance, had given them good service. 'We'll have to stop coming here,' Collins growled to his friend as they emerged into the street. 'She has us taped.' They went for a drink, and Collins, instead of returning to the office, escorted O'Sullivan to his. Again he dawdled, talking, and finally surprised O'Sullivan by telling him that he woud not return to Mary Street. 'There's something wrong there,' he said.

Lying on his desk in Mary Street were the personal possessions of Compton-Smith. Compton-Smith was a gallant British officer who had been taken and executed by Cork Volunteers as a reprisal for the execution of six prisoners by the British. Collins had tried to save him but was too late, so he interested himself in the return of Compton-Smith's belongings—a watch, cigarette case, ring and fountain pen.

He was already overdue for half an hour when the Auxiliaries dashed up the stairs. Miss Lyons, the typist, met them at a doorway on to the landing. As an Auxiliary pushed past her, covered Bob Conlon, and drew the door to behind him to protect his rear, she managed to pull it shut. Another Auxiliary, who kept her covered, demanded the key of the back room. 'We know Collins is in there,' he persisted. Then, distracted by what sounded like a scuffle on the landing above, he left her for a few moments, and in a daze she walked downstairs through the sentries and, although hatless and coatless, mingled with the crowds before the alarm was given.

O'Reilly was near the door when the Auxiliaries entered. As he cycled down Liffey Street he ran into Collins. They retired to the office in Bachelors' Walk. Collins guessed what happened. 'The game is up,' he said hopelessly. 'There's a traitor in the camp.'

A week before there had been a raid on the shop adjoining his other Mary Street office. Convinced they were coming straight in, O'Reilly had scrambled out of a back window on to a glass roof high over the street and gone clean through it. For some time he had hung with heels kicking and terrified women shrieking in the workroom below. Collins had watched the raid from a shop across the road. There had been the possibility that the Auxiliaries had come on regular information but chosen the wrong number. This second raid made it practically certain.

But Collins' suspicions went further. It was the first time O'Reilly had seen him rattled. He was deathly pale and agitated. Mrs. O'Connor, whom he visited later, had the same impression of him. He, who so rarely spoke, strode up and down the room, talking excitedly for over an hour. In Devlin's, alone with a friend, he broke down. 'There's a traitor in the camp,' he repeated hopelessly. To Batt O'Connor he said it was only a matter of weeks before he was captured. He kept on in a curious way, lamenting the loss of his own fountain pen. It is as though he were referring the greater to the minor loss.

But this was only to his intimates. With Miss Lyons he passed it off as a good joke. The British were now looking for Miss Lyons—they had found a dressmaker's account in the pocket of her overcoat—and Collins stood watching the next raid. He was the merriest person at tea in Mrs. O'Connor's that evening.

The Mary Street raid, or at least Collins' view of it, has never been satisfactorily explained. A strange story is told regarding it. After the Treaty a Castle official who was drinking with Collins began to discuss it. Collins interrupted him violently.

'I don't want to know!'

For himself, he obstinately maintained that he knew the informer, quoted the price paid him—£500—and commented bitterly on the fact that he had made a condition that 'there should be no bloodshed'.

Some settlement was now almost certain. Cope, the new Under Secretary at the Castle, a man whom Collins later learned to admire, was fighting the corrupt and crazy bureaucracy which was trying to squelch him as it had squelched so many other well-meaning people before him. Cope did genuinely want peace. Lloyd George had learned something since his previous experience and was prepared to negotiate in earnest, though he still sent out feelers and the same whispering nonentities visited the same backbenchers and huskily declared that a friend of a friend had said this or that. At the same time the English prepared to hang MacEoin.

MacEoin was ready to sell his life dearly. He was to be tried in the Hall in a long room overlooking Cork Hill. He arranged with Collins that at a certain point in the trial he would shoot down his judges and leap clean through the window on to a stone terrace forty feet below. Collins' men would lie in wait at the Exchange Hotel with a car and hustle off what remained. Fortunately he called it off.

The more savage the English grew, the more ruthless Collins and Headquarters Staff became. They have been blamed for it, as they have been blamed for failing to understand conditions in the country. Neither charge is just. If once the English had been able to show a slackening off of activity on the part of the Volunteers in return for any move of theirs, its effect upon the morale of the country would have been disastrous. Ireland was not a country organised for war. Several of the public bodies were only waiting the moment when it would be safe for them to rat.

It was equally easy for country Volunteers, fighting their own corner, to criticise Mulcahy and his 'paper work', but none of these had experience of the work entailed in getting hundreds of raw civilians, whom chance had thrown up as local leaders, to act and fight as an army with responsibilities outside their own parish. The Kilmichael ambush was one thing; the average Volunteer activity throughout the country another. This was the sort of report which sometimes cheered the heart of Collins and his associates:

'Work shown for a month. March was not up to much but April one much improved. We seem to be in terrible hard luck every thing goes against us. Batt. Comdt. No. 1 was ordered to reside in his own Batt. area and leave off drink. I issued orders to him to attack Police patrol in ———. He would not stay in his area did no cease drink. He went to

—— to attack patrol done nothing. Excuse made was cartridges would not go in guns.'

He still hoped to get X, a prominent inquisitor. Mac-Namara and Neligan, in their time at the Castle, had done their best to entice him out, and MacNamara, slapping him a little too heartily on the shoulder, had hurt his hand on a steel jacket. When this failed, they offered to kill him in the Castle itself, but on the occasions when the Squad got close enough to get X it was usually X who got the Squad. On one occasion he was followed to England and trailed about London, but the London men failed to make contact, and on his return the car which was to meet him at the boat broke down. On another Mrs. X had observed two suspicious customers outside the hotel where he was staying and rung up her husband, who arrived a few minutes later in a covered lorry to arrest his would-be killers.

The attempts to get Z and his gang were also failures, Z was a police sergeant who paraded the city with a picked gang of desperadoes from various counties. He had several shootings to his credit. On one occasion, when the Squad invaded Grafton Street to fight the gang, Z picked up two of them unarmed and made a pot shot of one. On another occasion, what would have been a wholesale clean up of Grafton Street —Z's gang, Auxiliaries, spies and all—was spoiled by some Volunteers who quarrelled with two Black and Tans and shot them dead.

And then the peace negotiations made de Valera so anxious to slow things down that the job was postponed, as well as the still more formidable one of wiping out the threescore Secret Service men whom Collins had now succeeded in locating in various parts of the city. They continued to pour in even after the Truce. One, met at the boat by Neligan and another Secret Service man, represented a New York newspaper. Scarcely had Neligan passed on this piece of information than the 'journalist's' card was presented to Collins with a request for an interview.

Collins actually met and spoke with a British Secret Service man, who liked him so well that he entertained the idea of asking Collins to assist him in securing information. Some secret Intelligence reports, in the preparation of which Collins gleefully assisted, were much appreciated in Whitehall for the inside knowledge they displayed of Volunteer activities.

Then suddenly Lloyd George abandoned whispering dupes and came out with a letter to de Valera. Now that the Ulster government had been formed he felt he was in a good position to bargain on an agreement which would exclude Ulster. De Valera replied, and a truce was arranged. The Wilsons and Frenches raged, the age-old Dublin Castle bureaucracy squirmed, but Cope had triumphed, and the Volunteers, the 'murder gang' of a few days before, became the Irish army, with whom British generals were required to enter into arrangements for the maintenance of order.

At a quarter to twelve on Monday the eleventh of July 1921, a slow procession of armoured cars, tanks and patrols began to return to their barracks, while doors and windows were crowded with sight-seers. It was a brilliant day. Summer was everywhere. The barracks gates opened. Noon began to strike from the city churches. One by one the officers and men filed in in full war kit, here and there with a cheer or a last hoot of derision. Those who watched will never forget the emotion of these scenes. These were not so much men and armaments as seven hundred years of tyranny, seven hundred years filled with more anguish than a world beside could show. Old men and women, remembering their childhood dreams, wept. The heavy gates closed slowly behind the British troops. In the streets of the city the people walked unmolested, joyously, incredulously, exultant in their acquired timidity. That evening they walked and talked till very late in the summer dusk. They had almost forgotten what an evening walk was like.

Collins sat on in his office at Harcourt Terrace, working.

PART THREE

THE TRAGIC DILEMMA

CHAPTER XIV

TREATY

No one who lived through it is ever likely to forget the summer of 1921. To some it seemed a triumph; to some, a disaster. Volunteer headquarters began upon an intensive campaign of organisation, recruiting, drilling and arming. All over the country summer training camps were established at which Volunteers were put through the usual paces of regular soldiers. British headquarters prepared for real war, gigantic concentration camps wholesale roundups. Collins went about the country interviewing local commandants, inspecting training camps, reorganising his Intelligence system. In Dublin he planned bigger and better gun-running, and during August the first shipload of arms reached Arklow.

Yet, for all the preparations for war, there was throughout the country far too great a feeling of confidence. It was only natural that this should be so; it was the British who had asked for peace; it was they who were humiliated when their officers were compelled to confer with Volunteer officers. Besides, it was the first time life had flowered here. Terrorised by landlords, bullied by policemen, magistrates and soldiers, shipped like cattle to the American boats, the people had never known their veins to run with pride before. There had been no leisure, no comfort, no communal gaiety. Now the killing weight of apathy and despair was lifted; it seemed to the young revolutionaries that a new world was beginning, a world in which their triumph must be embodied as an article of the constitution. As in France in the first days of the Revolution in which it was 'bliss to be alive', the impossible was made law. Wanted men appeared from nowhere and paraded their native towns, and loyalists and garrison looked on in impotent rage, and there began the deification of the Volunteers who had put up so fine a fight. Some fell to the temptation. Great fellows in uniform, all bristling with whistles and revolvers, they attended dances and public concerts; commandeered cars, ostensibly for Volunteer work, and tore up and down the little country roads with girls all the hot bright days of summer; stopped at wayside pubs and swanked.

It is hard to see how this could have been avoided. For years they had been hunted, slept in barns and ditches, or six in a bed in some shepherd's cabin in the mountains; they had been cut off from the society of women of their own class, from dances, pictures, theatres. It was scarcely in human nature that now, when life was returning to its old tranquillity, they should continue this underground existence, ready at an hour's notice to resume the unequal contest. Even the Black and Tan and Auxiliary, who had no reason to feel proud of himself, made whoopee. These were men, not saints, and they needed warmth and gaiety, kisses, sprees, dances and moonlight joy rides; all the more because they had so much to make up for. To most of them the years of fighting and imprisonment were like so many years stolen from their eager youth.

There was only one hope: negotiation, broad and brief, with the threat of war kept in Irish hands. But with de Valera that was impossible. A man who spent days over a newspaper interview could not be expected to conclude the issue of peace and war in one day. He must play for position. It would be October before discussions began, and December before the British took the initiative and said 'Sign this or——'. Collins realised the danger; so did his friends of the Republican Brotherhood, and they were confident that some compromise must be reached. Brugha, blind to this as to everything else, paid no attention. 'All we want you to do is to keep them talking,' he told the delegates.

In order to allow free discussion the British released all the imprisoned representatives with the exception of MacEoin. Collins replied with an ultimatum: 'No discussions without MacEoin,' and MacEoin was released that very evening. Collins was looking forward eagerly to seeing him, and when MacEoin entered the hotel and strode to the foot of the stairs

156

Collins was on the landing. With one bound he cleared the stairs and crashed clean down upon MacEoin, still suffering from the effects of his wounds, and pinned the unfortunate man to the ground.

He appeared at the meeting of Dail Eireann and was given a tremendous reception. Later he agreed to address his constituents in Armagh. The previous night he worked late preparing his speech, and when he left in company with his typist he was challenged by two armed men. He dashed his fist into the face of one and bolted, pursued by revolver shots. They were Volunteers on a joy ride!

Next morning he set off with his friend Boland for Armagh. This meeting was also a great success, and when the young man with the dark moustache leaped forward and threw himself over the platform rail there was a storm of cheering. As Collins warmed to his subject, people saw for the first time that strange fierce energy of his. He leaned forward, every muscle tense, the head tossing, jerking, the curved mouth twisting in a grin of scorn and defiance. But the tone of the speech was very different from what it had been in the days when he spoke in snowstorms in Roscommon. It showed how responsibility had changed the whole cast of his mind. 'The Orangemen,' he said, 'have been used as a tool in preventing up to the present what is now inevitable. The moment is near when they will no longer be of use as a tool, when they will, in fact, stand in the way of an agreement with Ireland, which has now become essential to British interests. Then they will be thrown aside, and they will find their eyes turned to an England which no longer wants them.'

The Orangemen retorted by ambushing him with stones as he pursued his way from Armagh. The Thompson gunner in the car looked longingly at his weapon, but Collins only laughed. 'Thompson guns aren't fair against stone,' he said. He was still the same larky youth. Boland and he indulged in endless horseplay, delighted to be together again. At three in the morning Collins was in his room, throwing the G.S.S.'s boots out of the window, and when the tyre was punctured the pair of them improved the occasion with pitch and toss.

Boland infuriated and delighted Collins with his Americanisms. 'Call that a meeting?' he asked in nasal tones. 'You should just have seen some of the meetings I addressed in Madison Square Gardens!'

Then at long last came what seemed to be the opening of negotiations and de Valera's announcement that he would not go. Worse than that, he ordered Collins to go. Both decisions perturbed Collins, particularly that which concerned himself. All his friends agreed that it produced an acute sense of misery and exasperation. He felt he was the soldier, the commander, and should be left at home while the politicians made the peace.

All that is true enough, but it does not explain everything. Collins' perturbation was more violent than the occasion seemed to warrant. Yet when de Valera had tried to send him to America he had refused to go. Why did he not refuse now? The reason for his perturbation and his surrender are both clear enough. He realised the very difficult position of his chief. At last the monstrous shadow of the Declaration of Independence was mounting above them all. After the Truce must come the compromise, and the question was how best to make it. De Valera reminded the Dail that he was not a doctrinaire Republican; refused to allow the delegates' hands to be tied by any instructions from the Dail; refused to allow anything like a discussion on the terms which the Dail might find acceptable, lest Lloyd George should get to hear, and proceed to whittle down the minimum—that imaginary minimum, one should say, for it was never defined until both Collins and Griffith had committed themselves to accepting less. He begged his followers 'not to mention the word Republic' and implored Griffith to 'get him out of this strait waistcoat of a Republic'. The drift of all this was clear enough.

Collins went to London 'as a soldier obeying his commanding officer', to use his own words, because he felt de Valera wished him to make concessions which de Valera himself, as President of the Irish Republic, could not in all decency make, but which Collins, with his secret society and his immense pull with the Volunteers, could not only make but persuade others to make. De Valera's ingenious scheme of External Association with the British Empire, as it emerged little by little from that subtle mind, he looked on as a way out of the horrible dilemma. It did not occur to him for an instant that de Valera's words and actions would be interpreted in a quite different way by others. This was only part of the mischief created in the cabinet by the open disagreement between Collins and Brugha. Collins went to London under the impression that de Valera was throwing dust in the eyes of Brugha and Stack and remaining at home the better to control them and get rid of the improvised Republic. Stack and Brugha believed that he was remaining at home to uphold the Republic and prevent Collins and Griffith from making concessions. One of the most amazing things revealed by the Treaty split was that none of the team of delegates and secretaries seemed to have the least notion what the other fellow was thinking of, and all were equally bemused when it came to the question of what de Valera and the rest of the cabinet at home intended. Mr. Pakenham considers that de Valera showed 'a great flair for preserving harmony'. I should have said 'a great flair for masking essential issues'.

Apart from his political responsibilities Collins had more personal matters to worry him. The girl he had been in love with for years married another man. On the night before her wedding he went to her hotel and pleaded with her not to go ahead with the marriage. Next morning he attended the wedding breakfast. Before he spoke he took out his handkerchief. When he finished the woman sitting beside him noticed that the handkerchief was in shreds. Collins was not the sort of man who could 'take love easy as the leaves grow on the trees'.

Collins did not like the London trip. It involved a certain number of social contacts, and four years of secret life had been a bad preparation for that. He had always been shy and rather self-conscious, hating formalities, most at his ease when he was with simple people. His companions noticed that he tried to dodge functions, and when it was necessary for him to attend any he was ill at ease. His clothes seemed to sit uncom-

159

fortably on him From every other point of view it was excellent that he should be there. He was the one spot of warm human colour in a rather colourless delegation, and photographers, pressmen and gossip writers delighted in him. His presence assured the negotiations a good Press. When he could, he indulged in the old horseplay with Dalton, Tobin, Cullen or any other of the old friends who happened to be there. As before, he was hammering at their doors in the early hours, drenching them with cold water, pulling the clothes off them, and wrestling on the floor in the old Stafford rough-and-tumble. But each morning he was also out to Mass, another sign that the Big Fellow was giving place to something much more formidable of character.

With his deep impressionability he cannot fail to have been stirred by the scene at Downing Street on Tuesday, the eleventh of October, when, after the wild cheering of the crowds, there came the opening of a door, the sight of a long room and a rosy, white-haired, cheerful little man who shook him by the hand and led him to his place almost opposite Birkenhead. It was a big change for Collins the Post Office clerk; a bigger change even for Collins who had crushed his shoulders all night against the buttress of Dominic Street church. None of the Irish delegation would have felt that magic but Duggan, and Duggan was a simple man. Barton and Duffy were not unfamiliar with this world; earnest, square, stolid Arthur Griffith would have sat down opposite the throne of the Almighty and argued the case of Ireland with the same lack of self-consciousness. Only he, with his artist's temperament, felt it all. He knew the English were holding themselves aloof from him, all but Birkenhead. With him there was an almost instant click, of realist with realist—the one young, fresh and unspoiled by ease; the other older, tougher, and coarser in fibre, but with a sense of reality which crashed ever and anon through the tissue of dialectic like a pile driver. 'I hate a slow mind,' he said feelingly, and Collins agreed with him. In such a crowd Collins was not at his best. He was happy only when formality had relaxed and the naked soul was showing. Against the stolid faces he would toss his airy

160

pleasantries and laugh louder than anyone else.

He had no confidence in himself as a diplomat, and the negotiations brought him many spells of deep unhappiness. He was appointed on to all the subcommittees, and here he could make his weight felt, as in anything in which he was given something practical and detailed to do. But though his presence alone added a reality to the conference which it would never otherwise have had; though the British, faced by the man with whom they really felt they had to deal, bid as they would never otherwise have bid; Collins was never so important a figure in the negotiations as his personality should have made him. This, too, is easily explicable. For Collins the discussions were to a large extent unreal, and that Pakenham does not sufficiently recognise this is the principal flaw in his brilliant analysis of the conference. Collins had trained himself to think exclusively in terms of power, and in terms of power the British had unanswerable arguments. Griffith and the others argued brilliantly, their tactics were often excellent; they were not so conscious as he was of the power of checkmate. Once, when the British had stood firm against some pet point of his, he raged in secret. 'If we had the guns there'd be no negotiations.' During the weeks that followed was being shaped the attitude with which he confronted Dail Eireann when the Treaty was an accomplished fact. 'Not freedom but the power to achieve freedom'—an attitude grossly misunderstood then and later. It was the realist's cry for power, any sort of power; something more disciplined than this army of shadows, this scarecrow treasury. From Collins' mental make-up it would almost seem as if every check should have made it more inevitable that he would compromise—and ensure a more certain comeback against those who had thwarted him. The negotiations were only just started when he sent James Douglas to America to inquire whether the new state would be in a position to borrow without complete fiscal autonomy. That is sufficient indication of his state of mind. Douglas noted that Boland was already preparing American opinion for a resumption of hostilities, which is sufficient indication of his.

161

Both Collins and Griffith put up as good a show as could be expected with de Valera's plan of External Association. Unfortunately for de Valera, neither took it seriously. Griffith had never concerned himself with the symbols of independence and was as ready to try and make a success of Ireland under the British Crown as under an Irish President. Collins was a different type.

At the source of all his actions were the old boyish emotions. At any moment they might have swayed him with a 'Fight it out'. An old song, the memory of a dead comrade, some traditional gesture of defiance, and he would have died as gallantly as anyone fighting on a Cork Hillside. But one had to appeal to Collins through the things he recognised. It was a different thing to ask him to die for de Valera's baby; and emotionally and intellectually de Valera's baby meant nothing to him. Again he was thinking in terms of West Cork and of the people and things he knew best. He did not give a button for the symbols over which de Valera worried. That sort of symbol was only the cachet of power. Judge's wig or bishop's mitre, these are only so much paper coinage which derives validity from actual resources. Given control of men, money and arms, Collins felt he could have all the symbols he needed.

But the other members of the delegation, Barton and Gavan Duffy, the landowner and lawyer, were familiar with the same symbols that worried de Valera. They saw the contrary effect of them; the way in which they refract the power they receive. Their ways of thought were different: Collins thought from the peasant up; these, from the monarch down.

The scheme of External Association (by which for Commonwealth purposes Ireland was a dominion; for internal matters, a republic) was submitted in various forms to the British, but without success. The British demanded recognition of the King; the Irish worked out a formula recognising him as head of the Associated States.

De Valera, writing from Dublin, said, 'There can be no question of our asking the Irish people to enter into an arrangement which would make them subject to the Crown, or

162

demand from them allegiance to the King. If war is the alternative we can only face it.'

'The first paragraph of this letter,' says Pakenham,* 'created a scene at 22 Hans Place. Griffith said he would go home unless the cabinet left their hands free. Collins was in a towering passion. He declared that those in Dublin were trying to put him in the wrong and get him "to do the dirty work for them".'

As Pakenham suggests, the towering passion was probably because Collins feared that he was being led into a trap by Brugha and Stack. But that is not the only reason. There is a strong probability that it was the first indication Collins had that de Valera was not exactly set upon a compromise. I believe that up to this he had been deceived into thinking de Valera was playing a deep game to remove the opposition of Brugha and Stack to any settlement whatever, and that this extraordinary sentiment from the man whose 'dirty work' he felt he was doing simply bewildered him.†

The explanation of De Valera's interference is much simpler. If meant simply that he was becoming more and more enamoured of External Association, which had the great merit of being all things to all men: a dominion to Lloyd George and a republic to Brugha, with all the symbols proper to a republic safeguarded. The trouble about the symbols was that they were rather new. The symbols the English were fighting

* Frank Pakenham: *Peace by Ordeal.*

† Since the publication of Rex Taylor's book it is obvious that I badly under-rated Collins' growing suspicion of de Valera. In a letter to O'Reilly written on the day of the first London Conference, Collins hinted darkly that his inclusion in the London delegation was 'a trap' intended to destroy his reputation in Ireland. As things grew worse between himself and Griffith on the one hand and the Dublin Cabinet on the other he became convinced of it, and of de Valera's part in it. 'I was warned more times than I can recall about the ONE,' he writes. 'And when I was caught for this delegation my immediate thought was of how easily I had walked into the preparations. But having walked in I had to stay.' But the nightmare of his suspicions did not cease there. From some of these bitter, anguished notes it is clear that he felt that what his enemies wished to destroy was not merely his reputation but his life. 'Got my political life at stake,' (Lloyd George) confided. I didn't answer him. 'My life—not only political—is at stake.'

for had the great advantage of being recognised; the average Englishman might be hazy about the exact meaning of Throne and Empire, but he would gladly have died for them. The symbols for which de Valera asked recognition were verbal formulae, with no tradition behind them, fired at the heads of the unfortunate delegation with instructions to see that they were recognised. But the two principal members of the delegation, who saw the symbols for the first time, were not so overwhelmed by their significance that they could cheerfully contemplate breaking off negotiations for them; it was in the highest degree unlikely that any but a handful of Irishmen would fight for them, and, forced to an issue, the Irish had no threat with which to sustain them.

There were things they could get; one of these was the unity of Ireland, and Pakenham shows brilliantly how Ireland was jockeyed out of that position. He also fixes the responsibility very definitely upon Griffith. But what does not emerge is that Griffith was jockeyed out of it because at the same time he was defending a position which he knew to be untenable. He would not break on the Crown. Pushed to extremes, neither would Collins. But they would break on Ulster, and it should have been the most important part of their tactics to show from the beginning that on that issue of the integrity of Ireland they would and could break; and that in breaking they would carry a united nation with them. Such a breakdown would have been understood anywhere, and the world's sympathy would have been with Ireland in refusing an Alsace-Lorraine within her borders. Lloyd George knew as much. There was little possibility of a breakdown on Ulster. England was fed up to the teeth with Ulster; the cabinet was sick of unionist advisers such as Wilson. It was perhaps only human that they should contrast him with a leader like Collins; soldier, student, man of the world. It is Wilson himself who tells of one extraordinary scene, when the Army Council gave a dinner to Pershing, and a cabinet minister declared that Collins was a better general than any of the English generals. When Wilson attacked him, he went one better. He said that Collins had beaten the English army.

164

Naturally there was a terrible scene and the cabinet minister was compelled to withdraw, but it does show how the cabinet had come to regard Collins on the one hand and the intolerable Ulstermen on the other; it shows how exact had been Collins' prophecy in his Armagh speech that the Orangemen would be thrown aside and find their eyes turned to an England which no longer wanted them.

The one thing the Irish needed to avoid was a break on the Crown because it would cost them the sympathy of the Dominions, and it was more than doubtful that Ireland would face war for it. They wanted the breakdown on Ulster, but for that very reason they had to shelve it until the tangled question of allegiance was disposed of, and the shelving of it convinced the British that they would yield on Ulster and gave them the very opportunity they needed of making a break on Ulster impossible. So, by elevating a minor obstacle to major rank and reducing the Ulster question to minor rank, they were playing straight into Lloyd George's hands.

In a short while the delegation was beginning to show signs of division. It had never been a happy family, because, whatever admiration Collins had for Barton, Duffy and Childers, it was an admiration for the extreme of himself (he showed it frequently, particularly with regard to his women friends); but it is a poor qualification in a task as difficult and dangerous as this was. The antagonism between Griffith and Childers was largely responsible. Griffith hated Englishmen, and he regarded Childers as an Englishman. He was rather unforgiving; silent, opinionated, unapproachable. Childers felt himself responsible for everything, from the secrecy of delegation documents to the behaviour of the typists; he was thorough, fussy, nervous. While he indited endless memoranda in that strange abstract way of his, his brows knit in thought, Griffith looked at him in dislike. 'There's that fellow writing more of those nonsensical memoranda and no one to take the girls to the theatre!' When Childers entered a room he shut up: he affected to believe Childers was an English agent. It was a pity, for in spite of Childers' overdeveloped sense of responsibility, which made him see Collins and Griffith as poor irresponsible provincials taken in by Lloyd George and Churchill (much as he saw the typists heading straight for perdition because they had stayed late at a party), he was by far the best-trained mind associated with the delegation, and a character of extraordinary nobility and purity; Barton loved him; admired him; his influence over de Valera was considerable.

Nor was everything at home as it should be. Brugha had decided upon a reorganisation of the army—heaven knows why, unless it was with a view to further weakening Collins' grip upon it. He hoped to place Stack as assistant chief of staff, though Stack had done nothing whatever in a similar position during the fighting. Headquarters wanted Eoin O'Duffy, who was Collins' protégé. De Valera suggested a compromise—there would be two assistant chiefs of staff. The conference between headquarters and cabinet broke up in anger. 'You may mutiny,' de Valera told them, 'but Ireland will give me another army.'

One army should have been quite enough. There were numerous breaches of the Truce on the part of the Volunteers —displays which were sheer braggadocio, with reporters and cinematograph operators; shootings, holdups, raids for arms. All these Collins had to account for over the council table to Lloyd George and Birkenhead, but when he held inquiries in Dublin, whole brigade staffs and even divisional officers conspired to deceive him and make investigation and disciplinary action impossible. In conference he pretended to make a joke of it: seized a rifle lying against the wall of the council room and gravely asked Lloyd George what this display of force might mean. But it was no joke. As a result of the peace, such grip as headquarters had had upon the Volunteers during the fight was slackening and the Volunteers were rapidly becoming a law to themselves.

Of course Brugha had to have a finger in the pie. In November he sent several young officers to London to raid barracks for arms; all this without informing Collins. They were soon discovered, and their arrest and imprisonment created a very bad atmosphere for the negotiators. Collins was

166

beside himself with rage. Again he felt the malignant influence of Brugha at work. Michael Hogan, one of the men arrested, preferred to face a British court rather than meet Collins in such a fury.

Yet in spite of work and worry he could find time to visit old Neil Kerr in prison, stuffing his pockets with cigarettes and liquor. He was cut to the heart when a warder intercepted them.

The split, which had been revealing itself little by little in London, came to a head at the cabinet meeting held in Dublin on the third of December, the week after Brugha's unfortunate attempt at collecting arms. The delegates came back with a draft treaty which Collins, Griffith and Duggan were prepared to sign, Barton and Duffy dissenting.

The issue had now fairly well clarified itself so far as negotiation could clarify it. The British had rejected complete independence in every shape and form. They would not have an Irish Republic. Neither would they have External Association with the British Empire. On the other hand, they had shown that they were prepared to concede Dominion Status with all it implied of future constitutional expansion. There was no further bluff; police, army, legislature—everything was to be handed over. To a practical administrator it offered immense opportunity. It is the sort of thing Collins must have dreamed of as a poor man dreams of financial security, independence, dignity and the chance of educating himself. Ireland could have these things, but in order to get them she must accept the suzerainty of a monarch whose authority she did not recognise. It was not a matter of adjustment; for a hundred years this evolving democracy had been moving further and further from the old Gaelic Jacobitism with its ideal of the Three Kingdoms. Fathered by the French Revolution, it had clung fiercely to the new ideal of an authority residing in the whole body of the people. It was a choice of tremendous significance.

Collins arrived in high spirits. After a lengthy wrangle, which lasted all day, he left in very bad spirits indeed. He grew angrier and angrier as the discussion went round and

167

round, an endless statement of purely personal conviction, with no attempt on the part of anybody to define the issue. Collins and Griffith felt that a practical maximum had been obtained; Duffy and Barton, that the British were bluffing and that they could safely go back on External Association again. De Valera could understand Griffith's bartering External Association for a United Ireland but complained he had got neither one nor the other. To Cullen, who drove with him as far as the boat, Collins complained bitterly of the way he was being treated. 'I've been there all day and I can't get them to say yes or no, whether we should sign or not.' He was not the only one who was dazed by that extraordinary meeting.

Next day Barton and Duffy were convinced that the cabinet decision had been to dish up External Association once more. Griffith and Collins were convinced there had been no such decision. Furthermore, they were satisfied that it would be utterly futile to attempt to go over the same ground again. Griffith agreed to go with the other two rather than allow the British to realise that they were facing a broken delegation, but Collins, fuming, refused point-blank to do anything of the sort. One can fully sympathise with his feelings. These proposals had been thrown out before. He had no desire to face another rebuff.

Griffith surprised the External Associationists. He put their case for them with all the weight and dignity he could command. They wondered at the superb integrity of the man. He tried to bring round the familiar break on Ulster, and for a time it looked as though he would succeed, but the conference collapsed upon a phrase of Gavan Duffy's, 'Our difficulty is coming into the Empire'.

'That ends it,' said Chamberlain.

Once again External Association had come in the way of Ulster.

The negotiations to all intents and purposes had broken down. Lloyd George asked for an interview with Collins and got it. Collins got to work on the British terms with no talk of External Association. His first point was Ulster. This was the thing which most worried him, and for Ulster he would

168

certainly have been prepared to make war again. The next was the oath, next defence and fiscal autonomy. On all these the British could and would negotiate. The conference agreed to meet again that afternoon.

At three it reassembled. After an certain amount of discussion it became obvious that Collins' interview with Lloyd George had borne fruit. Collins' Oath of Allegiance was accepted by Birkenhead, and the two realists must have smiled over it later, for it is a masterpiece of formula-making. And Lloyd George conceded fiscal autonomy, a more important thing by far from Collins' point of view, because he already knew from Douglas in America that without it it would be impossible for the new state to borrow.

Lloyd George then played his trump card: signature or war. Much has been made of it; rather too much one is inclined to think. The Irish had let it pass long before. After months of discussion it can scarcely have been unexpected. Why did Collins and the others not insist upon referring the matter back to the Dail cabinet? Griffith had pledged himself to do so; but how much that was plain to him, considering how much else had been left obscure, is hard to say. We have already seen the plight in which the Dublin cabinet had left the delegates two days before. Pakenham suggests that Lloyd George's artistry blinded the delegates to the existence of a phone to Dublin. It is much more likely they were blinded to it—Collins, at least—by that Saturday wrangle. There was little light there when the choice came to be made.

'I will give the answer of the Irish Delegation at nine tonight,' said Griffith, 'but, Mr. Prime Minister, I personally will sign this agreement and recommend it to my countrymen.'

At which, according to Churchill, Collins rose, looking as though he were going to shoot someone, preferably himself. 'In all my life I never saw so much passion and suffering in restraint.'

And so the delegates warred among themselves. Collins, Griffith and Duggan had put on their hats and coats to go and inform Lloyd George that they were ready to sign, but Barton and Duffy held out. Barton pulled the three men back, and

169

again the argument raged—the argument which, beginning in that room, would soon rage over all Ireland like a storm. Then Duggan broke down and described the hangman he had seen in Mountjoy (it had affected both his own mind and Griffith's). Barton caved in at last, and Duffy could scarcely shoulder the terrible responsibility of war alone. 'Mr. Prime Minister,' said Griffith coldly as they entered the conference room again, 'the delegation is willing to sign the agreements, but there are a few points of drafting which perhaps it would be convenient if I mentioned at once.'

It was half past two when they signed, and in the cold December dawn the five men returned through the silent London streets conscious that they had performed an action the consequences of which would be more profound and disturbing for their country than anything its history recorded.

Collins had no illusions about it. For him the trap had been sprung. He sat down to write to a friend:

When you have sweated, toiled, had mad dreams, hopeless nightmares, you find yourself in London's streets, cold and dank in the night air.

'Think—what have I got for Ireland? Something which she has wanted these past seven hundred years. Will anyone be satisfied at the bargain? Will anyone? I tell you this— early this morning I signed my death warrant. I thought at the time how odd, how ridiculous—a bullet may just as well have done the job five years ago.'

CHAPTER XV

A RIFT IN THE LUTE

DE VALERA heard the news on his return from Limerick to speak at a Dante Centenary Celebration in the Mansion House. The evening papers were just out. Stack showed him one. He glanced at it. Then Fitzgerald and Duggan arrived. Duggan presented de Valera with an envelope which the President brushed aside.

All Dublin, all Ireland, was now talking about it. In Hans Place Collins met a young officer of one of the Southern Divisions.

'What do you think of it?' he asked.

'It won't do for Cork,' said the young man.

Collins growled, the smile withering from his face. At such a time Cork must have loomed very great in his mind.

Next morning the argument which had begun in a room in Hans Place between five distracted men was transferred to every home and shop and workshop in Ireland. The objectors were still few, but they were vociferous—lads of nineteen and twenty, grown men with the inward-looking eyes of a Terence MacSwiney, women whose sons or brothers had been killed. They would never take an oath to the English king, they said. As yet no one paid much attention to them. Some older, more serious men were shocked by the exclusion of Ulster; they did not make such a parade of their sentiments, but their hearts were troubled and angry.

De Valera ordered the delegates back for a cabinet meeting on Thursday. Fitzgerald suggested that the summons might be amended.

'It reads as if you were opposed to the settlement.'

'And that is the way I intend it to read. Publish it as it is.'

At noon next day Collins and the others were at the Mansion House. It was only as the meeting went on that he realised the bitter truth: Brugha and Stack were opposed to the Treaty; that was only to be expected, since he was one of the signatories; but de Valera was on their side. Late that night they put it to the vote. De Valera, Brugha and Stack voted against the Treaty; Collins, Griffith, Cosgrave and Barton for it. After the meeting de Valera issued a statement which on Friday morning whipped up the argument throughout the country to a foaming fury.

Collins was beside himself with rage and anguish. O'Connor

171

gives a moving description of him that night standing at the door, hesitating, bitter, uncertain of his welcome—this instead of the old, bold, insolent swagger. 'I thought you would have no welcome for me, Batt,' he said. It does not even sound like the voice of Collins, so deeply is the man shaken, so uncertain now of every truth. At first he had thought all would welcome the Treaty except a few cranks or personal enemies like Brugha and Stack. Now he is prepared to believe that everyone will point him out as a traitor. He was certain that de Valera's influence would be sufficient to sway the Dail. The Treaty would be rejected and war resumed, with the Volunteers in their present plight, himself known, his men marked down. He planned to go to Cork and fight as an ordinary Volunteer with some West Cork column; in that terrible *bouleversement* he could not face the thought of resuming his old hand-to-mouth existence, with its intolerable strain and responsibility.

Next day he learned that things were not so bad as that, but bad enough they certainly were. De Valera's rejection had given new justification to the objectors; the Treaty was no longer a matter of disagreement, it was a test of orthodoxy. One was at liberty to call Collins and the others traitors. The objectors grew shrill; the waverers, certain. The Press was so emphatically in favour of the Treaty that its supporters might well consider its critics at least mad; though the discussion had gone on so long, it was not unpardonable to let one's temper get the upper hand and remember that one's neighbour had not always been so unblemished a patriot; his brother had been a soldier, his father a policeman; one distinctly remembered that at first he had not favoured the ambushes. Obviously he had a bad streak somewhere. And the middle classes were so pleased that the young have-nots of the Volunteers might lawfully suspect them of grabbing for place in the new regime. The women were the most hysterical of all. As society women had stopped young men in the streets of London a few years before and presented them with white feathers, so now they came to the young Volunteer officers and asked if they would prove themselves 'cowards' and 'traitors'; if they would give the lie to Tom or Joe, who had died by their sides, for a new Union Jack, a new oath of allegiance! When O'Reilly assured Collins of his devotion, Collins had only growled, wondering what it was all about. He was glad enough to receive the same assurance from Tobin and some of the others later. He realised now that there was a group, headed by Rory O'Connor, in the Volunteers which said it would never yield allegiance.

There began for him that argument which seemed as if it would never end. In Ireland life is still of the village; it goes on in public; slight questions of principle are exaggerated into village squabbes; all take part, as belligerents or peacemakers. Collins, with so much of the village lad in him, was peculiarly susceptible to this. He had the traditional respect for the person as person and expected himself to be held responsible in the same way; those who did not know the tradition complained that he turned every argument into a personal one. It was not the Treaty versus Document Number 2, but Michael Collins against his immediate critic. Add to this that he was deeply affectionate, unshakeably loyal, and one gets some idea of the hideous nervous strain which was now being imposed upon the one man in all Ireland who most deserved to be set free of it. Every disagreement, every assurance of loyalty, was a new burden upon that emotional nature. But there was worse than disagreement; there was the silent sundering of old friendships; the husband and wife who passed him in the street, the one smiling his love, the other turning away her eyes at the sight of the man she called a traitor.

Under the strain his iron nerve began to give way. His temperament came dangerously close to the surface. He grew unwontedly emotional even with strangers; tears came more frequently, more abundantly. Barton remembers coming upon a strange scene in a corridor of the Mansion House. Collins had been pleading with Childers. The two men stood facing one another—the big broad-faced country lad with the heavy jowl and the hanging lock of hair; the little English officer with the skeleton head and haggard face, 'sicklied o'er with the pale cast of thought'.

'Does this mean that we're going to part?' Collins asked.

'I'm afraid so.'

Collins crushed his fists into his eyes, and all at once Barton saw the flood of tears as he tossed his head in misery.

Well might they say he made every argument a personal one. And it was not only Childers. With all those who had meant anything to him, and they were many, there was the same drag of loss. He pleaded in tears for unity, sympathy, understanding, then, flying into a rage, dashed off with an oath.

CHAPTER XVI

THE GREAT TALK

ON the following Wednesday, the fourteenth of December, the Dail met and went into secret session. The same argument raged. After a few days it emerged from cover, and the argument was still going on. Behind the scenes each party was striving desperately for votes. Collins was paying the price for the zeal with which years before he had lopped off so many of the Hydra heads of moderation. It appeared to be a fairly equal division, with a few votes here and there swaying uncontrollably between one loyalty and another. As they checked over the list of deputies, one name gave Collins pause. 'Dishonestly for,' he pronounced at last, and then, as an afterthought, 'or dishonestly against.'

The Treaty debate was a staggerer not only for the world but for Ireland, and not only for the Ireland of yesterday but the Ireland of today. The gigantic improvisation was at an end, and from behind the scenes walked not supermen, not geniuses, but Lilliput in person, the same Lilliput which it seemed had caught its death in the snowstorm of the Roscommon election; the little Ireland of shopkeepers, solicitors and priests, with its parochial vanities and affectations; the Ireland which had blackguarded Synge, scoffed at books, let

Larkin down, believed it was all settled in the Penny Catechism.

Imagine a long room with fifty or sixty people crowded at one end—the public; inside a barrier, on a low dais, with his back to the audience, the Speaker; at his right, Collins, Griffith and O'Higgins; at his left, de Valera, Stack and Brugha. The rest faced him out. The Speaker was MacNeill, big browed, small chinned, yellow like some of his own mediaeval parchments, with hair almost identical in tone with his face.

Griffith moves the ratification of the Treaty; the little, cool, stolid journalist who had laid it all down in penny papers that hardly anyone bought. It was the occasion of his life. Had he been a dramatic type he could have told them of many days and nights of desperation, ignored by England and Ireland, listening in restaurants to young men chattering and laughing while his diligent humourless mind pursued its endless train of thought. He could have told them of his poverty and of those offers which would have made a rich man of him had he chosen to accept them. But he had no time for passion, for heroics or self-pity. A big man from the heart out, this Mr. Griffith, with his granite face, his papers, his orderly dispassionate mind.

After MacEoin had seconded him, de Valera proposed the rejection. His first words provide a characteristic nicety of thought. He cannot propose, he can only appeal. 'I tell you words mean [something],' he continued passionately, 'and in a Treaty words do mean something. They have meaning and they have facts, great realities that you cannot close your eyes to.' And again, 'Parnell was asked to do something like this—to say it was a final settlement. But he said, "No man has a right to set"—"No man can" is a different thing. "No man has a right," take the context and you know the meaning.' It was a pity that de Valera did not take the context because in fact Parnell said neither.

Stack follows, Collins' one-time friend and now among his bitterest enemies. Dull, pompous, unutterably futile, the threadbare sentiments string themselves out. 'This question of

175

the oath has an extraordinary significance for me, for, so far as I can trace, no member of my family has ever taken an oath of allegiance to England's king.'

After the luncheon interval Collins rises to speak. It is a good and manly speech, though not comparable with O'Higgins's or Beaslai's, but Collins, as I have said, was neither speaker nor writer, he achieved style only under compression in his dispatches.

Childers, still worried—more deeply worried than ever, for it is not only that poor boy Collins who is now going wrong, but a whole country—delivers a prophetic speech which is remarkable because all its prophecies have been proved false. As in London he had warned the amused typists against the night life of a great city, he warns the deputies against the perils of empire; it is the same fatherly tone, and like most paternal prophecies it sees only danger and losses ahead. It is followed by another prophetic speech, remarkable because all its prophecies have come true; the first great speech of O'Higgins, still only an untried young politician.

After that the proceedings degenerate into a mildly comic squabble. Sean Etchingham, better known as 'Patsy Patrick', rises. 'A lawyer of repute has said that that agreement that is now presented to us is couched in the very same language that Lloyd George mesmerised Wilson with. . . . The Free State, if you like, a bow window in the British Empire. . . . England never made a treaty she did not break. . . . He [Griffith] knows that I have read that in his writings in the *United Irishman* and elsewhere.'

'One deputy from Galway said that faithfulness meant equality,' expounds Joe MacDonagh. 'Well, I think that faithfulness does not certainly go so far, for in the Catholic Catechism when you make an act of faith in God you do not claim equality with God.'

'John Bull is not Almighty God,' retorts Sean Milroy.

Professor Stockley's speech shows a style like a sieve; the ideas he seeks to sustain sink gently down like fine sand through the holes in the syntax. 'Not even Mr. Gavan Duffy has said—in fact he has said the contrary—that the claim

176

made—and I would like to say it with regard to my present intentions on this Treaty—that the claim made that representatives of the people are incidentally to lose their own identity as it were—their own responsibility—and be no longer independent men because their constituents think something else—is, I think a claim that cannot be made, and I never heard it being so absolutely made to any assembly as this on behalf of any people.' One wonders how many assemblies Professor Stockley had belonged to.

Miss MacSwiney—whose three hours' flight of oratory, Mr. O'Kelly thought, put her 'in the highest ranks of the greatest orators of our race'—interprets the situation far better. She makes it plain at least that the issue is rejection or civil war.

Mr. J. J. O'Kelly takes occasion to point out that much of the disunion has been caused by speaking English and, breaking into English, proceeds to create more of it. The whole cabinet, he thinks, has drifted from the high plane it previously held to a slippery slope; and he appeals to the contending parties to turn their gaze towards heaven once more, and, hand in hand, to assist each other towards 'the exalted plane to which our cause has been brought by untold sacrifice of blood and treasure'.

Then in a noble speech Beaslai hit it off magnificently. He quoted Colum's 'the poor Irish nation striving to be born'. He saw in the Dail 'a body of small people, dry formulists and politicians, without imagination. We cannot rise to a great occasion. We haven't the vision.'

After this, one of the high spots of a disgraceful debate, there arose the airy, wandering Countess. She gibed at Collins by suggesting that he might aspire to marry Princess Mary, a suggestion that made Collins see red. His over-chivalrous protest hardly went to the root of the matter; that surge of rage had come from the consciousness that Markievicz was showing the snob in her, and Collins, with his sharp class sense, was caught on the raw.

The countess, faltering, had said, 'I have seen the stars.' J. J. Walsh said he had seen America. 'It cost me three pounds to get over and three pounds to get back. At any rate I have seen the continent of America.'

'Faith unfaithful to England's king,' said Mr. Fahy, 'cannot make us falsely true to republicanism. We are, as I have said, concerned with liberating our country from a dilemma and liberating a cat from a bag. The immense labour of the latter performance may give us some idea of the task before us.'

Mr. MacCabe, on the question of principle, read the Ten Commandments and challenged any deputy who had refrained from breaking them to stand up.

No wonder Collins, striding up and down the corridors of the National University, so often wore a moody and defiant look. No wonder that when one of the defenders of principle passed some slighting remark, he turned round with, 'Blast you, anyway, Ferran; you never did anything but introduce a spy.'

On the sixth of January de Valera returned with a staggering proposal. 'I resign,' he said in effect. 'Let us stop this futile debate. Re-elect me and I shall get rid of Collins and Griffith and face the English with Document No. 2.' It took the other side some time to realise that he was trying to change the issue from Treaty versus Document No. 2 to Griffith versus de Valera. Collins, in a rage, spoke of Tammany Hall methods, and his friend Boland, just back from America, was at his throat, though clearly the reference to Tammany Hall was not intended for him.

Seumas Robinson began promisingly. 'In my own plain, direct, if not too lucid way I would like to fire a few shots at this Treaty—metaphorically speaking. . . . To my mind this compromise has been lurking in the ante-camera of many a cerebrum for the past three years. . . .' He went on to suggest that Collins was not really the hero he was cracked up to be and, when sidetracked by the Speaker, who said this was as near not discussing the Treaty as possible, charged Collins and Griffith with having staged the final ultimatum and being guilty of high treason. He believed they should be grateful to him for saying so.

Collins' friend, O'Sullivan, was dignified and treated the House to a disquisition on Irish civilisation which should

178

'permeate and influence the life of every nation in the world'—
though the occasion was scarcely propitious.

Paddy O'Keeffe said he had Irish aspirations in his veins.
He spoke characteristically and well, though he repeated the
amazing statement that all the misunderstanding was caused
by the use of English, and then went on to speak English.
'Don't tell me,' he begged, 'that the Munster Fusiliers, my
own neighbours, didn't beat the Germans!' and in a striking
phrase compared Ireland to 'a bather perpetually in togs'. But
his best hit was in warning the Dail that they who were now
taunting one another would soon be killing one another.

Brugha stood up at last, the stormiest of Collins' enemies.
He had before him Robinson's queries regarding Collins,
asking what his rank was and if it could authoritatively be
stated that Collins had ever fired a shot at any enemy of Ireland.

The dirt was out at last! The Speaker did not intervene.
Collins welcomed the onslaught with a cheerful, 'Carry on!'
Brugha was out for fight. As happened always when he grew
excited, he burst into Irish. 'I'm going to say something now.
I'm determined on it, and if I'm interrupted I'm cross and
cranky. I'm no angel.'

'No one would accuse you of it,' Collins rapped out, in Irish
too.

Collins, Brugha declared, was only a subordinate in the
Department of Defence. The staff of that department had all
worked patriotically and well—all but Collins! Collins alone
had sought notoriety. He was made a romantic figure, a
mystical figure, such as *this person* is not.

Brugha's is a terrible speech. One can see the man in it;
stunted, gnarled, ruthless, with a hate like an old man's hate.
It created such an impression that two deputies who intended
to vote against the Treaty voted for it by way of amends. It
was listened to in dismay by Collins' worst enemies, in rage by
his friends. And yet there is something not altogether unattrac-
tive about it. At least it is all out; there is no reserve, no
restraint, no deception. One can see under all the perversion of
feeling and fact the man's fundamental honesty and integrity.

It is a man, to use a phrase of Æ's acting from his own will and centre. One cannot wonder that Collins continued to admire him.

Griffith's last words on the Treaty are the crowning achievement of his life; magnificent oratory. There is the same quality one finds in the highest oratory—the quality of an oath. It is man calling on God to witness. He began by a reference to Brugha's attack on Collins. 'He [Collins] was the man that made the situation; he was the man, and nobody knows better than I do how during a year and a half he worked from six in the morning until two next morning. He was the man whose matchless energy, whose indomitable will, carried Ireland through the terrible crisis, and though I have not now, and never had, an ambition about either political affairs or history, if my name is to go down in history I want it to be associated with the name of Michael Collins. . . .' Bitterly he went on to arraign some of the Republican members. 'I have an arrangement of oaths here, seven different oaths taken by different members of this assembly to the King of England. These were the gentlemen who unsheathed their swords against the liberties of the people—these gentlemen sat on English benches—all of whom are going to vote against this Treaty because they will not take the oath. Ah! this hypocrisy that is going to involve the lives of gallant and brave men is damnable—the hypocrisy of the men who hung their flags out when the King of England came to Ireland, the men who received him, the men who fought in his army, the men who sat on his benches—the men who try to cut down the brave young men of Ireland—this is damnable hypocrisy.' . . . 'I was told, "No, this generation might go down, but the next generation might do something or other." Is there to be no living Irish nation? Is the Irish nation to be the dead past or the prophetic future?'

Then comes the end of the Great Talk—it had gone on for weeks—and the vote for which all Ireland was waiting. As it is being taken Collins rises with a passionate cry. It is the voice of one on such a peak of emotion that he speaks already as if from the dead. At this moment he and Griffith are utterly at

180

one. 'Let the Irish nation judge us now and for future years!' he cries. The result: Sixty-four for, fifty-seven against. The Treaty is ratified. The war is over. Already from without comes the wild cheering of the crowds. De Valera grasps at his last straw, and in their triumph the others, not foreseeing the infinite mischief it will produce, let him have it. The Republic remains until the people disestablish it. Collins babbles like a boy. What are we, he asks, but a majority party and a minority party?—there's nothing more between us. De Valera holds the same position as ever in his heart. And then—out goes the hand in a gesture his friends know well, a gesture of monumental power, a Roman gesture—'my hand and my heart too'. The women at the back of the hall begin to sob violently, so suddenly does it release the springs of emotion. For a moment it looks as though de Valera will rise and take the proffered hand, but before he can do so, Cassandra shrieks. Miss MacSwiney is on her feet. The passion is still in the words, now colder than the clay of the slaughtered men. 'Let there be no misunderstanding; no soft talk, no *raimeis*, at this last moment of the betrayal of our country; no soft talk about union; you cannot unite a spiritual Irish Republic and a betrayal worse than Castlereagh's because it was done for the Irish nation.'

Collins, hurt and sulky, still begs for some basis of common action. De Valera has a last word of regret: 'Five years of magnificent discipline in our nation. The world is looking at us now . . .' and weeps. In the hush the voice of Brugha says that 'discipline will be kept in the army'. No more.

When they meet again, Collins, still a boy, is begging for his committee—a committee to take over from the English. He is in a wild hurry, there is so much to do; a whole world of new experience waiting for them all and they waste time in talking.

But the opposition has had time to harden. It refuses to assist in the disestablishment of the living Republic. De Valera resigns and is proposed and seconded for the position of President—of the Republic, that is. It is another move in the game. The Republic must carry on until the people disestablish it (it is strange that no one questioned that theory), the President must obviously be a Republican because you

181

cannot have a President subverting his own constitution; his cabinet of course must also be Republican in order to work in with him; so that naturally makes it impossible for Collins, Griffith and Cosgrave to be members! Meanwhile the Provisional Parliament would sit elsewhere, and de Valera thought it would be rather helpful to it to have a rival government.

One Republican member thought it disgraceful of Collins to propose such a thing as an executive committee instead of re-electing de Valera (though the disgraceful manoeuvre was intended to save him the humiliation of defeat on a vote).

Brugha speaks again. Clearly he believes he is telling the truth when he says that but for de Valera he and Collins could never have worked together.

Collins: That's true. It wasn't today or yesterday it started.

Brugha: I only wish we could be brought together again under his leadership. I only wish it was possible.

Collins: It is not though.

Collins gets ditherier and ditherier as the flood of evasions flows over him; he can make no head against the massed oppositions. Don't all the fighting men on the other side realise there is no essential difference between de Valera's proposals and the Treaty? Hasn't Mellowes said it was a case of Tweedledum and Tweedledee? Why, then, do they follow de Valera? At first he jokes about the new coalition. In the end he talks like a drunken man or a lunatic. 'Somebody will have to go to Dublin Castle and see what's there. Macready had to go to the Mansion House. They said I had breakfast with Lloyd George. I never had breakfast with Lloyd George.'

But de Valera has another quibble. The resources of the Republic must not be used to subvert it. Collins agrees. In that mood one might expect to find him agreeing to anything. He has the accounts ready. He will publish everything completely. He would prefer to publish everything completely. He is in a very difficult situation. People have destroyed their receipts. He would publish a notice in the papers, and when all the claims are in, if they are more than the total, some of the claims will be false—it is really a distraught man who is

182

speaking; in the disjointed phrases one can almost hear the beating of a human heart.

And so the game goes on. Griffith is trapped into stating that he will occupy the same position as de Valera had occupied if he is elected President. De Valera expresses himself satisfied. He takes it Griffith will do nothing to subvert the Republic, 'that you will do nothing which will make that Republic less a fact in the minds of the people than it is today'. In fact, that he will do nothing at all!

Miss MacSwiney does not seize upon this finesse. She wants two Griffiths, one forwarding the Treaty from ten to one, and another maintaining the living Republic from two to five. Poor Collins in his dithery fit had said something about having once hit an Englishman on the nose for jeering at Paddy and the Pig. 'My attitude,' said Miss MacSwiney, 'would be an attitude of the most intense superiority. I never knew anything like their impudence, and I told them so.'

De Valera then abruptly changes his mode of attack. 'I am not doing this through tactics of trickery or anything of that kind'—*but* Griffith had pledged his word to do what de Valera had asked him to do, and de Valera now opposes him on the ground that he could not possibly do it.

As though the cup of irony were not yet full, Patsy Patrick delivers another full-length speech. He refers to a typical homely phrase of Collins. 'The Minister for Finance gave us a pretty picture. I have often seen a team of horses under a plough. He wanted something to move the plough. What has he got? I have seen a team of horses galloping away from a gadfly. And who is moving the plough? Put Arthur Griffith at the handles, but Lloyd George is the gadfly that stung the horses. . . . God knows, this terrible warble, if it is not squeezed out, what amount of worms it will leave in the Irish people.'

Then, as the vote is being taken, de Valera rises and announces that, as a protest against the election as President of the Republic of a man pledged to subvert the Republic, he will leave the room. Collins seems to have been taken completely by surprise, and all the bitterness that has accumulated

183

in him during days of pricking and thwarting bursts out in one wild cry against this last damning proof that the unity of the people is broken. It is a cry of mortal despair.

Collins: Deserters all!

Kent: Up the Republic!

Collins: Deserters all to the Irish nation in her hour of trial! We will stand by her.

Markievicz: Oath breakers and cowards!

Collins: Foreigners! Americans! English!

Markievicz: Lloyd Georgites!

And this time the curtain really falls.

CHAPTER XVII

ALARMS AND EXCURSIONS

THE split, which was now handsomely under way, was Collins' peculiar tragedy and one which was a constant menace to his mental make-up. To begin with, he had no power of abstract thought; perhaps O'Higgins was the only man among the revolutionary leaders who had. What most of the others had was something very different: emotion disguising itself as abstract thought. When an Irishman talks of 'principle' he is a danger to everybody, because he has been brought up in an atmosphere in which the free play of thought is not encouraged. Collins' mind was obsessed with detail and he knew nothing of that myopia of the senses that enables a certain type of intellect to observe things in the mass, rather as a painter half-shuts his eyes to blur the clear obtrusive line. He did not understand the irremediable. It was a wall in which his temperament constantly sought to make breaches. It was probably the first time in his life he had not been able to translate that temperament ·into action of some kind. Those who accepted the wall were far from unhappy. They had their own private spleens to satisfy. Collins had none. Against the wall of hatred and misunderstanding his spirit went out constantly and vainly in a wave of anguished emotion. There is no use in pretending that Collins, if he had lived, would have acted as his colleagues did. The people say the contrary, and the people are right. In every action of his at the time one finds a terrible misery. It is only at this point that one becomes conscious that the Big Fellow of Frongoch has suffered another transformation; the passion for power has translated itself into what seems an absolute identification with Ireland. The man who during the negotiations had attended Mass every morning was already experiencing that identification. The split gives it an added urgency. The break in the life of the country is not something exterior to himself but a thing which rends his very being. That is how I read the cry with which he reproached de Valera on his final defection: 'Deserters all to the Irish nation in her hour of trial!'

That violent, Shakespearean emotion—swaying him constantly, making him now tearful, all surrender; now impetuous and scornful—rendered him a constant problem and danger to his political associates. On the fourteenth of January the elected representatives (de Valera's party of course absented themselves) met to elect a provisional government. Tied by his pledge to de Valera, Griffith could not be associated with it, so Collins was the obvious chief. Cosgrave arrived to find Griffith with a tragic countenance. In a cold voice he said, 'Mr. Collins does not see his way to proceed with the election.' In other words, Collins was prepared to scrap the Treaty.

When Cosgrave inquired the reason for this amazing change of front, it appeared that the British had been making difficulties about the release of some of the Irish prisoners in England. Cosgrave patiently explained that they were yet nothing but a party; they had no power to do anything for these men; given the formation of a government they could address themselves to the British with greater firmness.

'I agree,' snapped Collins as he concluded.

But his colleagues realised that the future of the state was in the hands of a very impressionable young man.

On the twentieth of January he signed a pact with Craig in

185

London, in order to lessen the bitterness which had grown up with Ulster and increase the chances of a Boundary Commission which would operate with the consent of both parties. The Orangemen continued to make savage attacks on the Catholics, and Craig promised to use his influence to prevent them, while Collins called off the boycott on Belfast goods. The pact lasted a little over a week. When Craig and Collins met in Dublin, Craig made it plain that not only was Ulster not coming in to the new state but that she would fight against any unfavourable decision of the Boundary Commission. Feeling was running high. Some Volunteers had been captured in the North, and it was proposed to hang them. Collins' warning that he would take reprisals was ignored, and he reluctantly closed his eyes to the proceedings of a group of Volunteer officers—MacEoin, Aitken and others. On the eighth of February they carried out a series of raids on Ulster and brought away a number of captives. Three days later a party of Ulster police, which by some mistake was diverted into Free State territory, was challenged by Volunteers. They replied with rifle fire, killing the Volunteer officer, and in a short while a number of them were killed. From this until the outbreak of civil war in the South, the Orangemen killed and burned wholesale. Almost every night a few Catholics—men, women and even children—were murdered. It probably began as an outbreak of religious fanaticism, but after a little while it became obvious that it was being maintained from higher quarters, in the hope that if it were carried out with sufficient savagery it might goad on the South to civil war and a fresh round with England. In the later stages it was likely that even British army officers were involved in a conspiracy to overthrow the Treaty and Lloyd George's government.

In an attempt to bring back some sort of unity Collins came to an agreement with de Valera at the convention in February. In the speech in which he proposed the conference there is the same note of pain which characterises so many of his later utterances. 'If they [the Republicans] can agree to go into conference with the Northern or the English representatives they can agree to go into conference with us.' He agreed to suspend the elections on the Treaty issue for three months to allow the Constitution Committee a chance of producing a constitution that would not give away the national position. Technically, it was a breach of the Treaty; practically, it was probably unwise, because the Republicans were arming and every week gave them fresh confidence; but the motive was the familiar one—unity at all costs. The British took alarm, and Collins and Griffith were called to London to provide an explanation. It is scarcely likely that they gave the real one, but even from the British point of view there was a sufficiently clear excuse in the fact that the new government was only a month in existence, had no army, no police force and could not possibly guarantee a free election. So Churchill permitted the suspended evacuation to be resumed, the uniformed Volunteers occupied more barracks and mounted guard outside the Bank of Ireland and the City Hall.

His visits to England were Collins' only escape from the gathering horror of civil war. The negotiations had opened a new world to him. He was always the learner. It had been the Childers, the Bartons, the Davies. Now it was Cope, Churchill, Birkenhead, the Laverys. He showed a new seriousness, though the old love of mischief for its own sweet sake remained; he still continued to say and do the utterly unexpected. At home in Dublin he had amused a tea table by announcing that the trifle was 'fine *dravuoil*'. At a tea party in London he handled the sugar tongs reverently, declaring it was a 'grand yoke', and removed the sugar lumps with cautious fingers from the claws before dropping them in his tea. There are many tales about his exploits in London. Some are probably apocryphal, but they show how he was regarded. The British admired him; he admired Churchill and particularly Birkenhead, and in one of his fine phrases he hit off that grim opportunist—'he was always loyal to the facts'.

At home he could only try to maintain so far as was possible the old relationships. Even if people would not believe him right, let them at least keep him as a friend. Even a few days before his death he was visiting in hospital a girl bitterly opposed to him in politics. Boland tried to do the same, and the two old cronies, after a drink and a wrestling bout, would roll home together in Collins' car. But Collins' place in Boland's mind had now been taken entirely by de Valera. It was the G.S. who could do no wrong. The G.S.S. made a joke of his new loyalty. 'I'm in a most unfortunate position, an international statesman out of a job.'

In fact Boland was becoming suspicious and resentful of his old friend. A curious story is told of them. One evening they were wrestling in Devlin's, and Boland got the worst of it. He stood back with a strange look at Collins. 'I see it now,' he said. 'You want to be a dictator.' It was a remarkable idea; psychologically, it seemed to me to have been quite accurate.

He surprised and shocked MacCartan by suggesting that, once entrenched in Dublin Castle, Collins would be as ruthless as any Englishman.

De Valera's policy was now one of obstruction, pure and simple. With unconscious humour the Dail Speaker, Mac-Neill, excused himself on the ground that 'continuous insomnia rendered him unable to stand the strain of presiding at the Dail meetings'.

Collins and Griffith played into de Valera's hands by allowing Dail Eireann to continue as a Republican Parliament until the Republic was 'disestablished' at the elections. As P. S. O'Hegarty points out, the proper course would have been to adjourn it *sine die* and summon the Provisional Parliament instead. The result was that ministers of the Provisional Government who had taken over departments from the British were questioned about these departments as though they were actually departments of the Dail and themselves ministers of the Dail. Obstructionist tactics were easy, because one could always ask if any other body dared to claim authority over the Dail; and each question provided a glorious opportunity for discussing the Treaty all over again.

Ministers of the Dail were approached to do things which they could only do by virtue of the powers and funds of the Provisional Government. If they did them they were betraying their trust as ministers of the Irish Republic, if they did not do them they were treating the Dail and their constituents with contempt. Griffith seems to have walked into the trap very easily, but when asked if the Provisional Government would be responsible to the Dail (which had not elected it), Collins snapped, 'Certainly not.' O'Higgins was exquisitely sarcastic and said that when he acted as minister of the Provisional Government de Valera's party looked on him as a national apostate, and in his capacity as national apostate he refused to answer questions in the Dail.

An ironic commentary upon this futile and tragic bickering was added by Lilliput, which waited outside the door in the shape of a deputation 're the censorship of films and the circulation of objectionable newspapers'.

De Valera then discovered that the register was invalid and that it was urgently necessary to give women the vote. The Irish people could not possibly vote upon the Treaty with such an imperfect register. Collins replied that they had voted upon the Republic with it, and that de Valera had never mentioned these difficulties when they agreed upon the three months' postponement of the elections, but nobody was in any doubt about the real reason for the move. De Valera wanted to postpone the election still further. He also made it plain that the Provisional Government must not attempt to establish a police force in defiance of the army. The army alone must act as police. As the army was the very body which made policing necessary, and as most of its officers refused to recognise the Provisional Government at all, this was pretty steep.

Within a week after that meeting of the Dail, the army, which was to police the country, showed its real temper. Though the Republicans had been organising and arming for months, the trouble began nominally over the occupation of the evacuated barracks in Limerick. It was the policy of the Provisional Government to allow all the British barracks to be taken over by local Volunteers, but in Limerick the local commandant had repudiated the authority of G.H.Q. Loyal Volunteers from another area were brought in for the job, but the locals resented this, and called in aid from their allies, the Republican Volunteers from the southern counties. For days the city was filled with hundreds of invading troops, who

189

marched and countermarched, followed about by busy cinematograph operators and watched by groups of British Tommies. It was largely bluff; they would have been unable to attack any large position, and, indeed, when it was proposed to do it O'Connor was shocked, but the bluff worked. There were parleys. On all such occasions the demonstration seems to have been solely with the purpose of starting a parley and declaring a truce, and, in most of these, excitable priests rushed from general to general, and the generals, straight from the paternal farms, sat at large tables and read maps and gave interviews; sometimes the two parties came to blows, there were shots fired and arrests made. Then there were fresh demonstrations and ultimatums, and fresh parleys and fresh newspaper interviews, in which the contending generals made it quite clear that it was the other fellow with his unreasonableness and bellicosity who was intent upon plunging the country into civil war.

It was the beginning of a campaign which would make the position of the Provisional Government intolerable, and but for its tragic consequences would have been exceedingly funny. It was not confined by any means to the Republican side. All the officers and men were young. They were not brigands, not murderers; there was nothing base or dishonourable about them, despite the propagandists on both sides. They were simply high-spirited, generous, adventurous boys, escaped from farms and classrooms in a country where all generosity, all adventurousness, all initiative and creative imagination had been ruthlessly suppressed for a century. They enjoyed the irresponsible romantic existence, the swagger which was made possible by a revolver or a rifle (thrice-happy the man who could carry a Thompson gun!), and the only blot on the picture was that the guns insisted on going off. Then there were parleys, handshakes, drinks, oaths of eternal friendship—and the damned guns went off again. They might, as the wiser among them suggested, leave the guns at home, but it is not so easy at the age of eighteen to throw off belt and bandolier.

It was only natural that Griffith should prohibit the holding of their convention, because only two days before they had shot Collins up in Cork; and two days after thrown petrol on his wagonette in his own constituency.

It was clear that they were out to hinder the election, and the next day made it clear that de Valera was supporting them. He made the famous speech about 'marching over the bodies of our fellow countrymen'; he has denied that it bore the meaning which most people attached to it, but a few days later the banned Volunteer Convention was held at de Valera's own headquarters. Rory O'Connor repudiated the Dail, and the new army, owing allegiance to its own executive only, was established.

This precipitated mischief everywhere. Local officers who objected to the Treaty now had an authority upon which they could rely and a sort of official blessing for any folly of their own. Collins discovered it to his cost when he went to speak at Castlebar on the second of April. The railway line was torn up; re-laid, it was again torn up; the roads were blocked for miles about with felled trees. Collins spoke in a storm of interruptions; the platform was rushed by Volunteers, one of his companions drew a revolver, there were revolvers drawn on the other side. The inevitable priest intervened to soothe wounded feelings. The Volunteers protested bitterly that they had not drawn their revolvers until Collins' friend drew his; they were merely rushing the platform in a strictly peaceable manner. Their officer jumped on the platform and declared the meeting 'proclaimed in the interests of peace'.

The rest of the month was filled with incidents like this. There were free fights about barracks; individual occupants whose allegiance—whether to the new Volunteer executive or the government—was in conflict with that of the majority were evicted. Sulking, they gathered together more of the same persuasion and forcibly occupied a post from which they could conveniently jeer at their ejectors. When 'incidents' occurred, each side issued long and contradictory reports showing clearly that it was the criminals, traitors and brigands at the other side of the street who were the aggressors, and that the saints of God at this had as usual suffered tortures and insults untold without complaining.

MacEoin endeavoured to stop this. The Republicans had occupied a hotel in Athlone, and he ordered them out of it by nine o'clock on the morning of Sunday, the ninth of April. At nine they were still there, and MacEoin surrounded them and took up positions ready for an attack. This looked serious, so a priest appeared and a parley took place. That evening the Republican Army marched out under arms, very gleeful. Two days later they returned and occupied the same hotel. Mac-Eoin issued another ultimatum, and again placed his troops in position; this time no less than four priests appeared. In a few weeks there was fresh trouble, and one of MacEoin's officers was killed. A third time MacEoin surrounded the rival garrison and issued an ultimatum; by this time feelings had grown heated; there was a danger it might prove serious, so the Republicans surrendered and gave interviews to the journalists, complaining that they had no other course open to them.

It was a gorgeous atmosphere of bluster and bluff. The Republican Army Convention met again on the ninth of April. A proposal to set up a military dictatorship was defeated— this looked likely to produce too much trouble. Instead, it offered to negotiate a peace on the basis that there should be only one government, that of the Irish Republic. This was done with a view to averting civil war. With the same patriotic and humane object the Competent Military Authority in Sligo prohibited the meeting which Arthur Griffith was to address there on the following day. The prohibition, he said, was 'solely in the interests of peace', and in the interests of peace the roads were blocked by trees and MacEoin's men had to cut a way for the President of the Irish Republic. The first government troops who arrived were met with rifle fire (also in the interests of peace)—they replied; there was a cessation of hostilities and the inevitable parley. It appeared that though hundreds of men had been drafted into the town the guns had gone off as usual without warning, so the fighting stopped and Griffith held his meeting, MacEoin and O'Connell swinging revolvers as they went along under the shadow of an armoured car, and the two armies eyeing one another belligerently from the windows of hotels and halls.

Collins came in for more of it when he went to Kerry a week later. The platform had been burned beforehand, and the Republican leader, accompanied by armed troops, warned Collins that the meeting would not be allowed. Collins went on with it unmolested. At Tralee it was discovered that some of MacEoin's men who had arrived the previous evening had been arrested by Humphrey Murphy's men. This was a favourite procedure, and the accepted reply was to arrest an equal number of opponents. MacEoin gave orders for this operation to be carried out and found the prisoners installed in his quarters when he arrived home that evening. Whereupon 'Free' Murphy arrived and protested against the arrest of his men; words led to blows, and MacEoin threw him down the stairs. He then jumped on him. MacEoin was surprised when a moment later a powerful arm descended upon him and he was thrown neck and crop into a tiny room, without even having seen the face of his aggressor. The door was opened again and an overcoat tossed in to him. Long after, the door opened and Collins appeared with a gleeful smile.

'So you're there still,' he said.

MacEoin followed him into another room. There was Humphrey Murphy.

'Now shake hands,' said Collins.

The two men shook hands. It was the beginning of a determined move on Collins' part to try and bring the officers together. He had failed utterly to come to any terms with de Valera and Brugha. Not only did de Valera always turn up with fresh suggestions for postponing the elections, but Brugha riled him. It was strange that Collins—whose tragedy would have seemed so inevitable, so fitting, in the black and savage winter of the Auxiliary campaign—was moving to his doom amid such folly and bitterness.

'Was it worth it?' he asked wildly of a Republican acquaintance. 'Was it worth it?'

'The Treaty wasn't worth it.'

Collins' head sank into his hands.

'No, and the Republic wasn't worth it,' he said bitterly.

CHAPTER XVIII

CIVIL WAR

THE negotiations which were taking place in the Mansion House broke down on the twenty-ninth of April because of de Valera's refusal to consider anything but a further postponement of the election for six months, 'to allow of a fresh register and the cooling down of the people's panic'. Collins had proposed a characteristically human solution: a Sunday morning plebiscite after Mass; but this the Republicans rejected as 'Stone Age methods'. Now the amusing little scene between himself, Humphrey Murphy and MacEoin in Tralee was justified, because from it, through the intervention of the Republican Brotherhood, came the proposal of a group of officers for a coalition government on the basis of a temporary acceptance of the Treaty position. On the first of May these officers appeared as a deputation before the Dail and begged it to do something to settle the split and check the drift towards civil war. Richard Hayes, replying, drew the obvious lesson and asked the Parliament to face the fact that 'the greatest movement the country had known was fizzling out in the greatest catastrophe it had known'. Hayes's attitude was typical of that of many on both sides who realised the immensity of the disaster but, though ready enough to face it at its most menacing, felt themselves entirely helpless in the midst of friendly Gilbertian armies and counter armies, proposals and counter proposals, truces, ultimatums and *voltesface*.

Thereupon the two parties selected five members each to form a Peace Committee. Whatever may be said of the Treaty side—and it is significant that Hayes's own name is missing—the names of the anti-Treaty representatives were proof enough that they would make no concessions. While waiting for its report the Dail continued to talk of the slump in trade, the anti-

Treaty group growing more and more indignant at the suggestion that the state of virtual civil war had anything whatever to
do with it. 'Really,' cried one of their number, 'the economic
life of the nation should not be mixed up with politics.'

Then the Peace conference returned, bearing a sword. In its
tragic and futile reports there are several touches of unconscious humour. 'Deputy MacGuinness commented strongly
on the fact that interruptions and abstentions had practically
left us without a full attendance at any time. . . . The committee, with the exception of Deputies Mellowes and Moylan,
who were not present, felt that Deputy MacGuinness was
justified in his protest.'

The tragi-comic discussions dragged on, while outside the
two armies battled to their hearts' content in an atmosphere
richly composed of earnestness, bluff and jealousy. On the first
of May a large contingent of Republicans arrived in Kilkenny
and occupied a number of buildings. These were retaken,
strange to relate, without loss. Next day Kilkenny Castle,
which was still in the hands of the Republicans, was stormed,
though on this occasion by some strange mishap several were
hurt. To show there was no ill feeling the government officers
had their photographs taken as they shook hands with the
Republican prisoners. Next day there was more fighting. And
still the Peace Conferences, which pious people insisted on
bringing together, kept breaking down because the Republicans could not see why Collins wished to implement the
Treaty at all.

In this atmosphere, on the twentieth of May, Collins signed
a pact with de Valera. It was a complete giveaway of the
Treaty position. There was to be no election on the issue of the
Treaty, there was to be a coalition government; the men who
had been tying themselves up in coloured ribbons of theory for
months past were to go on doing it for the future. Only one
concession did Collins wring from his opponent: that other
interests should be at liberty to contest the election. De Valera
was a hard bargainer.

It was even doubtful whether Collins' own followers
would not throw him over. There was a good deal of resent-

ment. Griffith, particularly, was stunned by the news, and his relations with Collins ever since the Treaty had been none too good. Griffith saw that the English demands were reasonable and that nothing was to be gained by ignoring them. When it came to a party decision the others squared up to the inevitable. They could not overthrow Collins. It came to Griffith's turn. He cleared his throat, removed his spectacles and cleaned them. He put them on again and adjusted his tie. Again he removed his spectacles and his hands were trembling. At last he said in a firm voice, 'I agree.'

That danger was past, but it remained to convince the English that an open breach of the Treaty at this stage was either necessary or advisable. Churchill denounced the Pact. The considerable and powerful group which was doing its level best to scuttle the Treaty in England denounced it. The supply of munitions to the Provincial Government and the evacuation were both suspended. Griffith, who was called with Collins to London, defended the Pact to the best of his ability. As on other occasions he had defended Collins' war policy against his own allies and the case of the External Associationists—which he did not believe in—he now pleaded for the Pact. There was a case there; that at least one must admit. The Provisional Government, for all its resources, had no real power. It could not, in the event of an election, provide even one soldier for each polling booth. This was the only way in which they could secure the people's approval—any sort of approval—for the Treaty. 'Griffith defended the Pact as though it were his daughter's virginity,' said one of his colleagues.

But the breach between Collins and Mulcahy on the one hand and their colleagues on the other was widening rapidly. Griffith, no longer young and with a life of struggle behind him, seeing the tardy fruits of victory snatched away by an impetuous young man who one day signed away the people's rights to satisfy de Valera and the next, diverted the Army, which should have been used to establish the people's rights, into a fruitless war for the defence of persecuted Catholics in the North, while he himself was labelled 'traitor' and marked down by assassins, plunged into hopeless heart-breaking melancholy. From day to day he expected the flash of the assassin's revolver; when he went to bed at night it was with the feeling that before morning he would meet the same doom that so many others had met—the reward for a life as selfless as any man had yet lived for the sake of his country. He was unable to stand the strain and was collapsing. Nothing could have saved him but one clear simple issue and immediate war. 'We must fight,' he cried passionately at cabinet meetings. 'We shall be disgraced in history as the greatest lot of poltroons who ever lived if we do not fight.' Collins would not hear of war. He, too, was suffering badly from strain and overworking to the point of a complete breakdown. He was losing the faculty of concentration. Now, when he was interrupted in his work, he could no longer transfer his wits with the same immediacy and precision.

The others who felt that Griffith was right were mostly younger men, but their connections had not been so much with the Volunteers. Hales, MacEoin, Murphy, Lynch, meant as little to them as Kelly the boy from Killann. Seeing the army now for the first time in the open they tended to despise it. Their minds were fixed upon an idea: the right of the Irish people to decide on the Treaty good or bad. To Mulcahy and Collins, who knew them at their best, the Volunteers were the people; they expressed what was best in them—their courage, tenacity and resourcefulness. The others, goaded by this new idea, were already beginning to forget their own indiscretions. Collins and Mulcahy remembered that they, too, had talked of a republic.

In a word, they were both 'weak' men, but Collins was a weak man his colleagues could not afford to ignore. He was still the Big Fellow.

They might decide what they pleased, but he went his own wild way. All they could hope for was his conversion. There were many conversions. Though his actions at this time resemble in their general recklessness the earlier Collins rather than the Collins of Black and Tan days, there was a new seriousness there. No one knew better than he that he was allowing himself to be led to the brink of the precipice. But the conversion lasted only just so long as Collins' mind allowed itself to be diverted into the abstract rights and wrongs. After that came the explosion. They came closest to converting him when the Cork Volunteers shut him out from the graves of the dead Volunteers. That stung him. He, more than anyone, had thought for those boys; he had toiled and intrigued to get arms for them, exulted when they were victorious, wept when they died. He had said there should be no more 'lonely scaffolds'. They were part of him as the abstract rights and wrongs were not. For a while his comrades saw him a leader again. He would assert himself. He would fight. But then came the grim realisation that he was planning to destroy others like those who were gone. His face was convulsed with pain.

'Ye're mad! Ye're mad!' he cried. 'Ye don't know what ye're doing.'

There is something tragic about those attempts of his to maintain the old loyalties intact. On one occasion a presentation was being made to Devlin. Collins was late, and everyone felt the strain. Republicans and Free Staters occupied opposite sides of the room; they spoke low; when they mingled it was with a certain formality. Collins, entering, sized up the situation at a glance. He bent, picked up a cork, and innocently flicked it into the face of a Republican officer, A little annoyed, the other returned it. In a moment corks were flying everywhere, and within five minutes the principal officers of the rival armies were rolling on the floor.

Collins, with his elasticity and brilliance, often forgot that these whom he looked on as heroes were sometimes vain, simple, uneducated men. They did not understand the demands he was making on them. He was asking them to rise above Lilliput; they were concerned with petty jealousies, with rank and precedence. Even within the new army, which was (more or less) loyal, there were endless squabbles. When yet another junior officer appeared at Beggars' Bush with the insignia of a general, Mulcahy protested to Collins.

'Ah, for God's sake,' growled Collins good-humouredly, 'let the bloody baby have his stripes.'

It would be impossible to exaggerate the genuineness and depth of his attachments to his old comrades, enemies and friends. It was as real as his crude sense of fun. When O'Hegarty was married, Collins' present was solemnly brought in during the wedding breakfast. It was a broken comb and a dirty toothbrush. But at the same time he snatched an ivy leaf from the table, wrote on it 'Diarmuid's Wedding, 27.4.1922', and, unseen by anyone, tucked it away where it was only discovered when he was dead. Long after, O'Hegarty showed it to me with a puzzled frown. 'Can you understand a man as sentimental as that?' he asked. I could.

But the split dug deeper and deeper furrows. Even the channels Collins had used for importing arms were now being used against him. 'By this time,' he wrote, closing an old account for ever, 'you will have seen where our opponents have led the country, and you must have seen that any "stuff" you may be sending them is being used, or will most certainly be used, for shooting down our own fellow countrymen.

'Believe me, the Treaty gives us the one opportunity we may ever get in our history for going forward to our ideal of a free independent Ireland. This cannot be gained without very much work yet—very hard work and perhaps more than hard work. And it is not by dissipation of the national energy that we can gain this. It is not by acts of suppression and it is not by denial of liberty that we can reach liberty.'

In a passion of love old Neil Kerr, who had seen the correspondence, began his next letter: 'My dearest Mick,' but the rent was in Collins' heart.

CHAPTER XIX

THE SHADOW FALLS

His enemies knew Collins' weakness to be his absolutely selfless loyalty and played on it. To one charge he could offer no defence—that he had let Ulster down. De Valera had done as much, but that was no excuse. Good men had fought for Collins there, and the politicians hinted that he was leaving them to the tender mercies of the Orangemen. 'Cannibal vengeance' was how Churchill described the murder of the MacMahons, and Collins, knowing his essential humanity, had tossed upon the council table the photograph of the murdered family. Churchill had wept. But while he and Collins disputed about the Pact in London a woman was set afire in Belfast and Dublin was swamped by fugitives.

The deputations who visited the Provisional Government from the North knew they had nothing to hope for from Griffith. To one such deputation he had replied in five words, 'Mr. ——, I know you.' On a later occasion when he was demanding at a cabinet meeting that authority should be given a prison governor to fire on rioting prisoners a Northern Irish bishop insisted on seeing him. 'I expect to meet Mr. Churchill,' said the Bishop. 'What shall I say to him?' 'What you think,' replied Griffith. 'Good evening.' He returned to the Cabinet meeting, pulling at his tie. 'Another damn fellow trying to dodge his responsibilities.'

Griffith realised the dangerous game into which Collins' pitiful, loyal temperament was leading him. Through Mulcahy he continued in touch with Rory O'Connor's men and encouraged them to armed intervention in the North—he gave them guns, impoverishing his own wretched little army which they themselves were challenging at home; he gave them men and diverted the energies which should have been used for building up the Free State into plans for a campaign in the

North. No wonder Griffith grew desperate. The whole Provisional Government was marching with a halter round its neck, and the halter was held up by Collins.

How hopeless the position in Ulster was is demonstrated by the bombardment of Pettigo on the fourth of June and of Belleek on the eighth. Catholics were being murdered in Belfast, but the British troops which should have protected them were being diverted into border battles against non-existent armies. The only enemies opposing the artillery on the border, wrote an English correspondent in indignation, were an English journalist and an officer guide. Collins insisted on an inquiry. He had no illusions about the responsibility.

'They were carrying out the policy of [those] who avowedly want to destroy the position created by the Treaty—to pave the way for the return of British troops and the ultimate reconquest of Ireland.' Ominous words which were to have an ominous sequel.

Passionately Collins longed for crises to stop and let him go on with his work—his own work: that of an administrator and statesman. One can see that he longed to tear down the whole fabric of Irish life and build it anew. He planned to bring back the Irish administrators from America and the Colonies and set them to work at home. It is a tragedy that he did not live to show what he could do, for his ideas, unformed as many of them are, have a quality alien to Irish politics. Since his death no Irish politician has spoken as he spoke about our towns and villages—'hideous medleys of contemptible dwellings and mean shops and squalid public houses'.

But there was no peace, and crisis followed crisis. On the sixth of June Griffith, O'Higgins and Kennedy went to London with the new Free State Constitution. It claimed the maximum liberty consonant with the Treaty, and in this Collins, as chairman of the Constitution Committee, was acting upon the advice of excellent lawyers. It was immediately rejected by the British who took the draft and altered it throughout, restoring the name of the King wherever Collins' advisers had informed him it might be omitted. On the face of it, if he accepted the revised draft there was no hope of unity with the Republicans; on the other hand, if he stood firm against the British he had no support to expect from the Republicans. On the twelfth Collins went to London and interviewed Churchill. Next day he returned and went straight to Cork.

The constitution crisis seemed to be the last straw. He was being attacked literally from every side. The British wanted the strictest interpretation of the Treaty, whether or not it involved him in war with his old comrades; Griffith more or less supported this view. De Valera wanted the Treaty issue set aside for another six months, if he would allow it to go before the people at all; Wilson and the Unionists wanted to scuttle the Treaty and the whole Irish nation with it; they, he felt, and Churchill in a speech seemed to support the view, were responsible for the ship of arms which so fortuitously allowed itself to be captured by Republicans off Cork; Liam Lynch and the Volunteers wanted the skies, and when Collins spoke in Cork on the fourteenth he may have known that even such negotiations as were being conducted between Lynch and himself were to be broken off next day and what amounted to a declaration of war against the British made from the Four Courts. Some such feeling stole into his speech at Cork. His opponents read it as a repudiation of the Pact. It is doubtful if it was intended so, because next day he spoke again in favour of it; but there is no doubt that some violent emotion, some feeling of the utter hopelessness of his position, made him urge the people to take the matter out of his hands. Perhaps it would have been the wisest course to have taken from the start. Minor battles and truces, theories, interpretations and broken agreements must have made it clear that this Pact, too, was quite unworkable. No one had defined what the Pact Parliament was to be, whether it was to be a Republican Parliament or the Parliament provided for under the Treaty; an all-Ireland Parliament or one for the new state; no one could guarantee that the army would obey it or even recognise it. Even before the election results were announced the Republican Army Executive was discussing the renewal of war with the British under an army dictatorship. Liam Lynch opposed it; so did Brugha. There was a clean break, the considerable minority which insisted on war retiring and locking themselves into the Four Courts. Having repudiated Mulcahy, they now repudiated Lynch. Much hope there was for the Pact, with a *coup d'état* in the air!

It was in this atmosphere that Collins, half demented, was receiving Reggie Dunn and discussing the killing of Henry Wilson. The murder of Wilson is an extraordinary business. When I wrote this book originally I believed I could see some explanation of it. I believed—as Collins certainly did—in Wilson's implication in a conspiracy on the part of English extremists to make the Treaty unworkable and produce a new and bloodier reign of terror in Ireland. But even admitting this, Collins' behaviour is almost inexplicable. Not only was he behaving dishonestly towards the English Cabinet, he was behaving dishonestly towards his own. For the first time he was making himself responsible for a killing which had no conceivable earthly authority to justify it, and allowed men under his command to run the risk of perishing without even that poor gleam of honour that has lit so many a 'lonely scafford', to use his own moving words. What are we to make of a man who allows a hero like Dunn to die an infamous death without accepting public responsibility for his own part in it?

No one can help wondering whether, as with American gangsters, killing hadn't become too easy to him—the simplest way out of any difficulty, but regardless of prejudice, this is very difficult to believe. Apart from his particular gifts Collins was a very ordinary man; one might even say a conventional man. His ideals were genuine but they were simple. He was not particularly ruthless, as revolutionaries go, and he was not lawless; he had far too much of the country boy's respect for what people thought.

Indeed, this very conventionality of his may well be the reason for his dangerous and crooked behaviour at the time. He was a conventional man who had been deprived of his conventions. For the first time in his life he stood completely alone. He was being attacked by the British Government for not implementing the Treaty, by his Cabinet colleagues for the same reason; by the Unionists for having achieved the Treaty and by the Republicans for having signed it. If he stood by his pledged word to the British he must kill old friends and comrades, which to a man of his temperament must have seemed monstrous; if he didn't he was guilty of treachery to Griffith and his associates. Collins simply did not have the temperament to stand alone: Griffith did, Brugha on the other side did. It is almost as though in having Wilson killed he was seeking for someone to blame for a tragic dilemma that was only in himself. And he knew the madness of it. For the first time he did not discuss the Ulster business, with its armed interventions and assassinations, with any of his advisers. He knew they would round upon him and rend him for his sentimentality, and this time there would be no defence. He was arming himself against reason. Yet life went on. On the twenty-first, while Dunn and Sullivan were preparing for the last act of their own tragedy, Collins was enjoying himself at MacEoin's wedding. He stole MacEoin's old pipe as a gift for Jimmy Santry, knowing how the Cork blacksmith would treasure that memento of another of the trade, and MacEoin received a handsome Kapp and Peterson to make up to him for the loss. It is a characteristic bit of sentimental thoughtfulness, like his treasuring of the ivy leaf from O'Hegarty's wedding breakfast; all the more so because death was in the air.

On the twenty-second of June Dunn and a companion named Sullivan shot down Wilson outside his own door in London. A crowd followed them; Sullivan, a veteran of the Great War, had a wooden leg and was unable to stick the pace, and Dunn gallantly remained by him until both were taken.

The cabinet heard the news and were appalled. They had no idea that, thanks to Collins, the hothead, the sentimentalist, they might be involved. It was only long after that some of them began to suspect the truth. Griffith issued a vehement repudiation. Rory O'Connor did likewise. De Valera was cautious and statesmanlike. Collins' immediate concern was to save the lives of two brave men. He had never yet let down a comrade. Cullen was sent across to London with instructions to get them out at any cost, by force or bribery; he was to pay any price, take any risk.

But the terrible drama was drawing to a close. When Cullen reached London he found that there was absolutely nothing to be done. The British had taken every precaution to ensure that the two men did not escape. Lloyd George wrote instantly to Collins, pointing out that documents had been discovered on Dunn and Sullivan connecting them with the Volunteers, that the Four Courts was about to resume the war; and insisting that the situation there be brought to an end. Collins at this time was in Limerick, but those in Dublin sent a temporising reply. There is evidence that the British were themselves thinking of attacking the Four Courts to assuage the anti-Irish fury which Wilson's assassination had provoked.

On the twenty-fourth of June the election results were announced. In spite of the Pact, in spite of personation and dragooning, the Republicans had lost twenty-three seats and would have lost more but for those left uncontested by agreement. His colleagues noticed a decided change in Collins. Always a man of the people, the people's judgment gave him new heart. 'Still, I wish we had the Bishops against us,' he said.

The Sunday which intervened was the last day of peace Ireland was to know for a long time. On Monday the House of Commons denounced the Provisional Government, and the director of the Belfast Boycott in the Four Courts raided Ferguson's garage in Lower Baggot Street with the double object of suppressing trade with Belfast and securing transport for the Republicans' punitive expedition to the North. The Treaty forces were called in and Henderson was arrested. That night the Four Courts men, following out their old policy of maintaining face, arrested General J. J. O'Connell, the deputy chief of staff of the Government Army.

What was the Provisional Government to do? Arrest another Four Courts officer? Or release Henderson? Either would have been an admission of incompetence. At midnight on Tuesday they served an ultimatum on the commandant demanding the evacuation of the Four Courts before 4 a.m.

No one has yet offered a reasonable explanation of the events leading up to this decision. On the same day as the ultimatum was issued Churchill had said in the House of Commons that 'The presence in Dublin of a band of men styling themselves the headquarters of the Republican Executive was a gross breach and defiance of the Treaty. . . . If it does not come to an end, if through weakness, want of courage, or some other even less creditable reason it is not brought to an end, and a speedy end . . . we shall regard the Treaty as having been formally violated.' That is what Republicans rely on when they say that the ultimatum was issued at Churchill's command. But members of the Provisional Government deny it and say that, far from being an incentive, Churchill's speech had a contrary effect and almost decided them upon taking no action at all. And, for various reasons, the explanation seems inadequate. In itself, Churchill's speech, and Lloyd George's letter which had preceded it, were not sufficient reason for initiating a civil war four days before the meeting of a new parliament. Neither Lloyd George nor Churchill had shown himself unfriendly (indeed, having regard to his training, Churchill's attitude throughout a difficult period was fine); given any reasonable guarantee that the matter would be brought before the new Parliament, they would not and could not have taken action.

The more reasonable explanation is that the Provisional Government realised that for months it had been barking up the wrong tree, and, perhaps too hurriedly, decided to make good the time it had lost. Some such realisation had certainly been in Collins' mind when he advised the electors to take the issue out of his hands and vote for whom they pleased. With that was the fear that the minority in the Four Courts, foiled in their attempt to initiate a general Republican attack on the British, would attack them alone, involve others of their comrades, necessitate British reinforcements, and—final humiliation—compel the Provisional Government's troops to fight side by side with the British against them. That, as well as being an immediate danger, would also have been a temptation. The Republicans were hopelessly split. The Four Courts minority had banged their gates in the face of Liam Lynch their own chief of staff; deprived of his assistance, and that of his followers all over Ireland, they might be driven out of the Four Courts, and fighting would not spread outside the streets of Dublin. And again, if they put off the evil hour, would they be likely to get as good an excuse for war as the arrest of their Commander-in-Chief? O'Connell was popular; the Free State was not. The soldiers might fight for their favourite officer, but there was no guarantee that they would fight for so shadowy a cause as elective government.

As usual, Collins, uncertain, was throwing all his weight upon the side of peace. To Mulcahy, the one man with whom he was spiritually in contact, he declared they must fight. But when it came to a decision he opposed it. Churchill's speech had exasperated him. 'Let Churchill come over and do his own dirty work,' he snapped. But he was in no position to stand pat and refuse to allow the army to be used. He, more than anyone, was responsible for the position in which the government now found itself. It was he who had made all the concessions, and at the end things were worse than ever. Had he been sterner then, he might have been more emphatic now. And if one considers what waiting for Parliament involved, one realises the depth of futility to which the Government might have sunk.

So the ultimatum was issued and received, and the government were not aware that Liam Lynch had returned and spent the evening in the Four Courts, or that its garrison was again prepared to recognise him as Chief of Staff!

Collins retired to Greystones for the night. At four the attack began. He arrived in Dublin next morning to find the station invested with troops and fighting in progress. He heard the boom of the big guns, tolling out the doom of the great cause he had carried to victory. It was a still, cheerful summer morning. Crowds had gathered to watch the shells crash against the robust dome; the quays were lined with curious sightseers. From the outskirts of the city little groups of men with rifles and revolvers gathered in to occupy posts of vantage. They were Republicans mobilising. Among them was de Valera and

207

Brugha. Collins and Boland met for the last time when they called at Vaughan's Hotel for their laundry. Collins, as usual, was in tears. Everything had the casual, inconsequent air with which life and death are invested by Lilliput.

Boom! boom! went the guns all day. The scattered seagulls screamed above the Liffey, flying higher and higher in widening circles. From the roof of government buildings Griffith watched the bombardment. Despairingly he shook his fist at the clouds of gun smoke and cursed de Valera.

CHAPTER XX

APOTHEOSIS

IT was Friday before the Four Courts garrison surrendered. In the meantime Lynch, who had issued in Dublin a fiery proclamation calling Republicans to arms, retired to Cork 'to rouse the country'. He roused the country, but, instead of rushing to the relief of the Four Courts and the other buildings in which his men were besieged, he went off to Limerick. There, having engaged the garrison, he offered in the usual fashion to negotiate a truce. In the usual way it was agreed to. But Collins, having once set his face to the hard road, was having no more truces. The priest was told to clear out and the Republicans ordered to evacuate the town, which they did. It showed the temper of their resistance.

After a week of fighting they surrendered in Dublin. In the blazing wreck of the Hamman Hotel Brugha fought on like a lion. He had already nerved himself for the last ordeal. He had never retreated from the English; he would not retreat from his own countrymen. There is something about his end which recalls the old sagas. He ordered his men to surrender. Alone in the blazing building, he made his choice to die by gunfire. Miss Macardle describes how his men, standing with their guards in a little lane beside the hotel, anxiously asked one another what had become of him. 'Suddenly they saw him in the doorway, a small, smoke-blackened figure, a revolver in each hand raised against the levelled rifles of the troops. Enemies and friends cried out, "Surrender." But, shouting "No!" Brugha darted forward, firing, and fell amid a volley of shots.'*

When Collins heard the news he wept.

Soon enough he had cause to weep for another death. Trapped in his hotel in Skerries, Boland, always prepared to take a desperate chance, bolted down the corridor from his guards. A sentry raised his rifle, and he fell, shot through the abdomen. When he died Collins came into Fionan Lynch's room crying helplessly. It seemed as though there would be no end to the slaughter of old friends.

Collins took on his new job as Commander-in-Chief with the usual intensity, even if there was no joy in his work. It was not the old army which had beaten the Black and Tans: hasty recruiting had made it in part a haphazard collection of wasters, ex-British soldiers, people with whom he had nothing in common. Within a fortnight five hundred of them had surrendered their posts and arms and been packed back to Dublin. There was a general feeling of apathy and hopelessness. The exchange of courtesies between old comrades went on; men changed sides from day to day. Against this Collins warred. Devlin describes calling on him at eight in the morning at Portobello and seeing him wave a hopeless hand at the deserted barrack square. 'Not a soul up yet.'

When Dublin had surrendered, Kerry was the next point of attack. Some of his old comrades pressed Collins to try and secure peace now, before more blood was spilt and fresh passions engendered. 'Let us take Cork first,' he said. He merely wanted overt evidence of victory before opening the negotiations. Cork was taken, and with it the position of the Provisional Government was made secure. Collins set out to inspect the occupied posts. He was in Limerick when he heard of Griffith's death. He had been washing his face in the morning when he collapsed, a blood vessel broken in his brain.

* Dorothy Macardle: *The Irish Republic.*

In fear for the future of his country, he had been going to pieces. He died a peculiarly lonely unknown man, as poor as the first day he entered Irish politics.

While he walked in Griffith's funeral Collins knew these were the last hours on earth of Reggie Dunn and Sullivan. They cannot have been far from his mind. In Wandsworth Prison they were awaiting the hangman and a death of infamy, while Collins walked, with his staff behind, as head of the Irish Government and the Irish Army. He had never looked finer. A murmer of delight rose from the crowds as he passed. At the same time Dunn, who by one word of disloyalty might have saved himself, was enduring the last utter humiliation. For each it was apotheosis: for Collins the crowds and the adoration, for Dunn the condemned cell and the shame. On the morning of the sixteenth of August he and Sullivan were hanged. Collins had still a week to live.

He lived it in suffering, mental and physical. Though still full of ideas and enthusiasm, he found it hard to work. He sat at his desk, scribbled a few lines, then rose and left the room, not in the old dashing way but slowly and in dejection. The shadow had begun to fall. To Cosgrave he said, 'Do you think I shall live through this? Not likely!' He turned to a typist and asked, 'How would you like a new boss?' It was so strange, coming from him that she repeated it to O'Reilly who worried over it. Next day, as the two of them were driving into town together, O'Reilly asked after his health. 'Rotten,' replied Collins. There was a slight pause. 'How would you like a new boss?' came the question. O'Reilly's heart sank. He replied that he would never work for anyone else. Collins smiled, a queer half-smile, but O'Reilly saw he was gratified. Though he still bawled down solicitude, he was obviously grateful for it.

He promised to see the peace envoys on his return from Cork. His staff was under the impression that in his native country he hoped to meet some old friends now in arms against him and add their influence to the cause of peace. That was also the impression he left on Thornton, whom he sent to prepare Clonmel for a conference by withdrawing all but old

Volunteers from its garrison. Thornton was ambushed and shot down on the way.

On the night before his departure for Cork he went to bed at 7.30. He was suffering from a bad chill. O'Reilly and his batman stuped his stomach. O'Reilly then went for oranges and made a drink for him. 'God, that's grand!' he sighed. Encouraged by these, the first words of gratitude that had passed between them, O'Reilly went so far as to tuck him in for the night. But this was too much. Gathering all his strength, Collins bawled, 'Go to hell and leave me alone!'

Next morning at breakfast he was still very ill—'writhing with pain', Mulcahy describes him—but absolute in his determination to get to Cork. He roused a friend to say good-bye and joined him in a farewell drink.

'You're a fool to go,' said the other.

'Ah, whatever happens to me, my own fellow countrymen won't kill me,' said Collins moodily.

O'Reilly woke at six and, moved by some impulse, rushed to the window. Collins was standing outside on the steps waiting for the armoured car to arrive. He wore a small green kitbag over his back, his head was bent in gloomy meditation, and O'Reilly thought he had never seen so tragically dejected a Collins as this man who, thinking himself unobserved, let himself fall slack in the lonelines and silence of the summer morning.

The instinct of devotion was strong in O'Reilly. He pulled on his trousers and, indifferent to rebuffs dashed downstairs to say good-bye, but the car was already gone.

Ill and distraught as he was, Collins went on to Limerick and from there to Cork. On Monday he saw friends and people with whom he had business. In the evening there arrived an old friend of Frongoch days. Collins sprang to his feet, delighted, and had the room cleared. He pretended to believe that his friend had come to ask for a commission in the army. But the friend did not agree with either side. He thought they were all mad.

Collins fell serious at once. They argued, pulling the threadbare theme to and fro again. Collins' love for men was so much greater than his love for ideas that it did not weary him as it would another. His friend pleaded earnestly for agreement, any sort of agreement that would save the nation.

'Very well,' said Collins. 'See me tomorrow night. I may have news for you.'

His friend interpreted this as a hope that he might be in a position to negotiate with some of the Republican leaders next day, or at least was in touch with someone who might. Then he noticed the old mischievous gleam in Collins' eye.

'And now,' said the Commander-in-Chief, 'what about a bit of ear?'

He pulled off his tunic with lightning glee.

'I will not,' said the other, scandalised. 'What would the sentries do if they saw me wrestling with you?'

'They'll do nothing at all,' said Collins. In a moment the Commander-in-Chief and his friend were rolling on the floor.

Next morning, as he stood in the lounge of the Imperial Hotel chatting with Dalton, the hero of the Mountjoy attempt, he saw another old friend, Pat MacCrea, his driver, pass through the hall. MacCrea had been ambushed and wounded in Wicklow.

'Ah, Pat,' he said, 'your fellow countrymen nearly did for you.'

He set out with a party under Dalton. They passed through Macroom, Bandon, Clonakilty, Rosscarbery, Skibbereen and Sam's Cross, where years before he had recited 'The Lisht' for the neighbours. They crowded in again to shake his hand as head of the Irish Government.

It was evening before they struck the back road from Bandon to Macroom. An ambush party had been waiting there since morning. Now, with the failing light, they scattered to their billets, and as Collins' convoy tore up the narrow road through the glen there were only a handful of men left. They opened fire. Dalton shouted to the driver to go like hell. Collins countermanded the order; the cars screamed to a halt, and he leaped out with his rifle in his hand. For close on half an hour the fight went on. Collins continued to fire until the little group of ambushers took to flight. He followed them with his rifle. All at once Dalton and the others noticed that he had ceased to fire. They thought they heard him call. When they rushed to where he was lying they found him, his head resting on his arms, a great wound in his skull.

O'Connell whispered the Act of Contrition into his ear and dragged him across the road into shelter while Dalton continued to fight. Dalton then came and bandaged the wound. He had scarcely completed the task when he saw that Collins was dead. Darkness was coming on. O'Connell was weeping. Dalton still supported the heavy bleeding head upon his knee.

The glen was quiet again, only the wind stirred in the bushes. Over all a wild and lovely county night fell; the men came in from the fields, gathered at the crossroads for a smoke, sat about the fire where soon they would say the rosary; clearer in the darkness sounded the wheels of the little country cart thumping over a ledge of stone, a cart such as Collins had seen and thrilled at in the Shepherd's Bush Road. But he would hear it no longer. The countryside he had seen in dreams, the people he had loved, the tradition which had been his inspiration—they had risen in the falling light and struck him dead.

Ireland had still to learn the news. In the early morning a middle-aged man was knocked up at a house in Lansdowne Road. Two or three young men stood on the steps with faces like death. They had come to tell the middle-aged man that it was left to him to carry on the task their chief had begun. . . . There was a crowd in Government Buildings where the Provisional Government was isolated behind sandbags and barbed wire. A door opened and two young men came in: O'Reilly and Cullen. O'Reilly, still half asleep and unable to take in the news, was ready for any trick they might play on him. When they saw the grey frightened faces the two lads burst into loud unrestrained weeping. Cosgrave stepped forward, his index finger raised. 'This is a nice way for soldiers to behave!' . . . Two doctors went across Stephen's Green. The dawn was breaking. From close by they could hear the crash of the snipers' rifles; they were going for an embalmer. . . . In the

213

morning a steamer set off from Dublin to bring the body back. It passed another steamer flying the new state's colours at half-mast, and heeled about, bringing up the rear. There was wild talk of a massacre of prisoners by way of reprisal. Mulcahy, rightly interpreting the dead man's thoughts resumed the negotiations where his death had broken them off. But he did so unknown to his colleagues. The day of lofty ideals was over; an evil twilight full of storm and sinister shadows succeeded that long day, too long and bright for Lilliput's cross and weary eyes.

It seemed as if life could never be the same again. The greatest oak in the forest had crashed; it seemed as if it must destroy all life in its fall. It did destroy the Sinn Fein movement and all the high hopes that were set in it, and a whole generation of young men and women for whom it formed a spiritual centre. It destroyed the prospect which, we are only just beginning to realise, Collins' life opened up: fifteen years —perhaps more, perhaps less—of hard work, experiment, enthusiasm; all that tumult and pride which comes of the leadership of a man of genius who embodies the best in a nation.

But life can stand many things, even the death of a genius. The historical process is not defeated, and through hatred, despair and apathy we are approaching, however slowly, that enthronement of life which is the goal of every historical process before fulness spells its end. It is not our tragedy nor that of the heads of government or the soldiers. It is the tragedy of men who must go through life marked indelibly by their contact with magnificence. Collins had spoiled them for lesser men. They would be quick, too quick perhaps, to feel the cold touch of normality, and Collins' death left normality enthroned.

Admirable normality! Lilliput needed a rest. Genius is a troublesome bedfellow. When it is absent we sigh for it, when it is present we grow weary of its violence and impetuousness. O'Higgins once said, 'I have done nothing without asking myself what Michael Collins would have done under the circumstances'—which is as though I were to say, 'I have written nothing without asking myself what Shakespeare would have written.'

What can normality do but keep the bed warm till her troublesome bedfellow, his night-wanderings over, returns, and she, forgetting how she had called God to witness her sighs and groans at his betrayal, looks again with alarm at the rugged frame, catches the breath scented with wine and that subtle odour in the hair which suggests strange contacts; till the eternal, restless marriage is renewed, and new generations, new ways of thought, are in the womb again?

INDEX

216

hurling, 18–20, 54, 125
Hyde, Douglas, 17

I

idealism of Collins, 23, 65, 184–5, 203
India, 65, 85
insurrection, 22, 25–33, 36, 43, 47, 62
Intelligence Service, Collins's, 72–4, 79–95, 97–100, 116, 117, 120–2, 134, 138, 142, 151–2, 155
Irish language, 16, 23, 24, 35, 57, 65, 75, 113–14, 176, 179
Irish Parliamentary Party, 40, 45, 48, 55–7, 64, 129
Irish Republican Brotherhood, 36, 38, 40–4, 55, 59, 61, 67–8, 98, 116–17, 128, 139, 156, 158, 194
Irish Self-Determination League, 85

J

'Jameson, Mr.', spy, 85–92, 94
Johnstone, Col. W. Edgeworth, 83

K

Kapp and Peterson, Ltd., 89, 204
Kavanagh, Joe, 33, 48, 57, 66, 71–2, 116
Kelly, John of Killann, 120, 197
Kennedy, Hugh, 201
Kent, David, 184
Kerr, Neil, 79, 106, 128, 167, 199
Kerry, 142, 193, 209
Kidd's Restaurant, 92, 118
Kilkenny, 195
Kilmichael, 127–8, 150
Kimmage, 27

L

Labour party, 129
Lanigan, Steve, 22, 70, 128
Larkin, James, 17, 174
Lavery, Sir John, 62, 187
Lenin, 71, 106
Leonard, Joe, 146

Liberal party, 129
Liberty Hall, 27, 30
Limerick, 85, 170, 189, 205, 208–9, 211
Lincoln prison, 59–60
Lindsay Road, 136–7
Liverpool, 70, 79, 106, 128, 130
Lloyd George, David, 45–6, 48–9, 55–6, 59, 94, 100, 103, 128–9, 142, 149, 152, 158, 163–6, 169–70, 182–4, 186, 205–6
Loan, National, 64, 75–6, 101
London, 15, 18, 20, 22, 33, 46, 54, 85, 141, 150, 157–70, 185, 187, 196, 200, 204
London-Irish, 18, 20–1, 27, 29, 31
Longford, 41
Lord Mayor of Dublin, 68
love, Collins in, 41, 159
Lynch, Fionán, 5, 31, 42, 209
Lynch, John, of Kilmallock, 122, 124
Lynch, Liam, 119, 197, 202, 207, 208
Lyons, Alice, 5, 143, 147–8, 157

M

Macardle, Dorothy, 11, 208
MacCabe, Alec, 178
MacCartan, Patrick, 96, 188
MacCrea, Pat, 5, 146, 212
MacCurtain, Tomás, 94, 100–1, 107
MacDermott, Seán, 22, 24–7, 29–33, 34, 36, 79
MacDonagh, Joe, 49–52, 176
MacDonagh, Thomas, 24
MacEóin, Seán, 120, 141, 143–7, 150, 156–7, 175, 186, 192–4, 197, 204
MacGarry, Seán, 49, 60
MacGrane, Eileen, 134
MacGrath, George, 5, 26
MacGrath, Joe, 26
MacGuinness, Joseph, 195
MacKee, Dick, 43, 75, 120, 122–7
MacMahon family, the, 200
MacNamara, James, 73, 86–9, 118, 125, 136, 138, 147, 151

219

222